Always in Season:
Folk Art and Traditional Culture in Vermont

Always in Season:

Folk Art and Traditional Culture in Vermont

Edited by Jane C. Beck

This exhibition was organized by
the Vermont Council on the Arts
and made possible by grants from
the National Endowment for the Arts,
the National Endowment for the Humanities,
the Cecil Howard Charitable Trust,
and the IBM Corporation.

Always in Season: Folk Art and Traditional Culture in Vermont

Published by the Vermont Council on the Arts, 136 State Street, Montpelier, Vermont 05602

Library of Congress Catalog Number:
82-70924
ISBN: 0-916718-09-3

Participating Vermont Institutions:

Vermont Historical Society Museum, Montpelier
May 8, 1982 –
November 1, 1982

Shelburne Museum, Shelburne
January 15, 1983 –
March 7, 1983

Christian Johnson Memorial Gallery
Middlebury College, Middlebury
March 20, 1983 –
April 25, 1983

Bennington Museum, Bennington
May 6, 1983 –
September 15, 1983

"Gathering Christmas Berries"
1978
Lee Hull,
South Royalton, Vermont
Oil painting
31½" L x 22¾" H
Loaned by Lee Hull

Every fall the Hulls used to go up to Swanton with their family to gather berries and balsam for their Christmas wreaths, a small business that he began in 1932 and which has prospered and is continued by their children and grandchildren. The first year the Hulls were unable to return to Swanton due to their failing health, Lee painted this picture to recapture the enjoyment of those fall days.

8.

Maple Sugaring Scene
c. 1910
Unknown, Vermont
Wood
17″ H x 42½″ L
Loaned by the
Shelburne Museum

Acknowledgments

Three years ago no one could have imagined the scope a general survey of Vermont folk art would take. Without the help and tireless energy of a great number of people and the support of the Folk Arts Program at the National Endowment for the Arts, the Museum Program at the National Endowments for the Humanities, the Cecil Howard Charitable Trust, and IBM Corporation, there is no way that a catalog could have been prepared or an exhibition designed.

First thanks go to the fieldworkers who helped locate the objects: Nora Groce who worked in southern Vermont; Kim Guay who focused on the Franco-American community; Karen Lane who visited various Italian, Russian, Polish and Swedish communities; and John Moody who conducted research among the Native American population. They did their jobs well and gave the selection committee over 2000 slides to choose from.

The selection committee composed of David Dangremond, Elaine Eff, Scott Hastings and William Lipke worked tirelessly, discussing, questioning, probing each item considered, and in the end agreed wholeheartedly on the final selection. They merit a warm vote of thanks, as do various consultants who added their expertise all along the way. Fred Fried, with his vast knowledge of folk art, took time away from a heavy schedule to help suggest, locate, and advise on various matters. Kristina Bielenberg and Barbara Van Vuren each lent her special expertise — Tina on the subject of brown ash basketry and the Sweetser family, and Mrs. Van Vuren on the subject of butter molds. Gordon Day spent time going over slides and giving sound advice on Abenaki material. Rayna Green not only located a number of Abenaki objects, but acted as general advisor on all the Native American material.

Bill Hosley, Gene Koshe, Ruth Levine, Ranney Galusha, Edmund Steele, Mary Labate, and the entire staff at both the Billings Farm Museum and the Shelburne Museum have given willingly of their time and information. Elaine Eff went far beyond her role as curatorial consultant and has had a major hand in guiding this project to completion.

Then there are those who have taken time from their Christmas holidays to write the essays: Wes Cate, Scott Hastings, and John Moody and those who have struggled through various parts of the catalog, giving valuable criticism: Bob Baron, Horace Beck, Elaine Eff, Suzi Jones, Duane Merrill, Linda Morley, Meg Ostrum, Nike Speltz, and Lee Huntington. And just as important is the typist Lucille Collins.

The cast of characters goes on: Erik Borg, photographer, his capable assistant Katherine Kennedy, and Mason Singer, designer, are all important in bringing the catalog about. And without Dan Mayer, the exhibition designer, there would be no exhibition — just a mass of objects.

But most of all my thanks go to the many many people who took the time to talk to other fieldworkers and myself, to give us leads and to show us their own pieces of folk art. From these people come the lenders to this exhibition. Without their generosity and patience none of this could have come to be.

Jane C. Beck
Vermont Folklorist

Foreword

Always in Season, Vermont's first folk art exhibition, is in many ways the culmination of three and a half years of research and documentation by the Vermont Council on the Arts and Folklorist Jane Beck. When the state arts council started the Folk Arts Project we wanted to know who were the authentic practitioners, those singers, quilters, carvers, basketmakers, loggers, story tellers and others, who carry the past into the present. We wondered if one could discern and demonstrate "quality" and "art" in these folk ways. And most of all we wanted to decide if the traditions we assumed to be a profound part of Vermont's character really exist today, or are instead part of a myth perpetuated by the nostalgic among us. This exhibition offers a simple and resounding affirmation: our traditions are changing, sometimes threatened, yet they exist all around us, binding us to our heritage and to each other.

This project, more than any other initiated by the Council in its seventeen years, tells about the people of Vermont. **Always in Season**, illustrates our history, our patterns of settlement, our natural resources and our occupations. It's about our self-reliance, our pride of work and craftsmanship and even about our poverty. The uncelebrated folk artists in this exhibition are people who responded to necessity by making things in a way that goes beyond "making do." A coverlet made of bleached grain bags and lovingly embroidered becomes more than a warm covering for a winter's night; it is also a pleasing design and a sample of family pride.

Most of the objects in this exhibition have functions in daily life: ash baskets to carry produce, fish jigs for ice fishing, rugs for floor covering. Yet they are made with such individuality, such liveliness, such creativity that beyond their usefulness they also tell about their makers' need for beauty — a need as persistent and urgent as the inventiveness of necessity.

This exhibit is organized into three general categories: the Native American Heritage, Farmstead and Family Life and Rural Occupations. These are the groupings which suggested themselves as the researchers looked at the several thousand pieces that were found and documented. Other organizing ideas may also have served, for example, to display the objects according to their materials such as fiber, wood or clay. How to define "folk art" and categorize it among other creative expressions is indeed one of the issues raised by this exhibition.

The essays in the catalog will raise more questions. They represent the individual, sometimes idiosyncratic, ideas of the writers — people who have thought about these things and their makers and their relationship to the rest of us. I hope their opinions are provocative and help you see deeply.

Many thanks are proffered in these pages; such a monumental effort needs many workers. I will add a few more. Jane Beck, Council Folklorist with her endless vision and energy is the foundation of this project. The Council trustees who supported this initiative — an unusual one for a state arts agency — also deserve thanks, especially Violet Coffin, Council President, William Lipke, Art Historian and Exhibition Advisor, and Lee Huntington, editor. Nothing would have happened without the belief and backing of the Folk Arts Program of the National Endowment for the Arts, Bess Hawes, Director. And the exhibition would have been impossible had it not been for the enthusiasm and support of the IBM Corporation, Essex Junction, Vermont.

Now we must turn this exhibition over to you, the audience, and seek your participation and enjoyment as the final recognition of the maker's vision and the collector's eye.

Ellen McCulloch-Lovell
Executive Director
Vermont Council on the Arts

Slate Fan
1908
John Benjamin Evans,
Poultney, Vermont
Slate
19″ H x 19″ W x 7″ D
Loaned by the
Bennington Museum

Preface

Imagine the task of organizing the visual record of centuries of Vermonters who have chosen to express themselves through available materials despite a lack of formal training. I can think of no more enviable job than to scour the cities, villages and countryside of the Green Mountain State in search of her indigenous arts and artists. The job of the folklorist is to locate, document, preserve and present traditional culture wherever it may appear.

The organization of an exhibition of the tangible arts of a specific place is comparable to the completion of a many-pieced puzzle. However, unlike a jig-saw or crossword puzzle with finite limits, the pieces here are unknown in advance. Only upon completion can the full picture be discerned. There is only a skeletal framework of minimal rules and barest clues to be followed. No handbook, map or key provides the procedure for engaging in a search of this type. The tips are in the landscape, guarded by institutions and people who are the makers or the caretakers for this season's or ages-old creations.

The completed puzzle is an accumulation of stellar objects that in the final presentation are mute. Behind each object is a person, a community or an individual, and a story. Each piece of the puzzle represents a chain of communication that leads the fieldworker-detective closer to some imagined end. It becomes his duty to find the traditional arts, whether still in the workshop of the maker, displayed on the walls or shelves of a loved-one's home, set out in a shop or flea-market for sale, already placed in another environment, or shelved in a public space or in the bowels of a cultural institution's storage facility.

Once located, the object must be reconnected with its past, so that it provides a meaningful link in this multi-dimensional puzzle. The human factor is, of course, the most significant. Conversations with artists or their kin are the folklorist's mother-lode. It is through such dialogue that the work of art takes on the meaning with which it was originally imbued — and without which it might be merely a mute witness to a never fully understood history.

Rather than being presented finally with a series of orphaned artifacts that reveal little about a place or time, the objects that have been assembled constitute an instructive chapter in the history of Vermonters' creative expressions, allowing us to see how Vermont views and portrays itself through the eyes and hands of her own people.

A new tangible sense of the state emerges from the survey that was conducted over a period of several years. Specialists in ethnic, native American arts and rural trades and crafts joined the quest to identify Vermont in another form. In a sense the search was taken up by all Vermonters as they were summoned to join by local newspapers and informed at regional public forums that their material heritage was vital and sought. This puzzle rather than being the work of a single "detective" employed the entire force. Everyone became a "suspect" as well as an informant. In infinitely flexible roles as makers, owners and admirers, every Vermonter is involved here.

Since 1976 almost a dozen states have attempted to seek and present their folk artistic treasures. Each of these impressive efforts allows us to assess a state's sense of itself. Just as in early geography lessons, when students are faced with a map of the United States that pictorially represents the industrial and natural resources of a certain area, we could now redraw that map pin-pointing specific folk expressions. We can also begin to reevaluate naïve notions that there is an "American" folk art that is found universally.

Instead what we happily discover is that the urge to create, despite a lack of formal training, is in fact an historic and continuing American tradition; that certain forms endure, others die, some are revived, some newly introduced; but more importantly that certain areas and individuals because of their locations, religious and political beliefs, surrounding land forms, climate and native materials provide as well as nurture all the basic necessities for a special type of art object.

Vermont is the first New England state to investigate this long continuum of artistic endeavor from its settlement to the present — to realize the value of last winter's painting or assemblage, while considering it on the same level as an eighteenth-century family record or bed rug, despite a relentless change in technology and literacy.

By its very nature folk art is inclusive, so much so that it often includes the work of individuals who may not even be aware of their status as folk artists. Because we identify this expressive material as a movement outside the canons of art history or Renaissance standards, we may find the dabbler, the creator by necessity, or the artisan included in this definition.

In the same way that Vermont's arts reflect active moments in the daily life of its inhabitants, it comes as no surprise that this rich output should read like a three-dimensional almanac given life by its makers. At this point the objects begin to speak for themselves, as we see Vermont recreated in visible form.

To write the book on folk art, preconceiving the categories of endeavor and materials, would be a great mistake. As we see here, **Vermont tells us** what are its concerns and preoccupations through materials that originate and thrive in her own natural landscape.

To reconstruct the puzzle that ultimately reveals Vermont's indigenous arts, it is necessary to sample her natural resources in the same way that Vermonters discover them while going through the motions of daily life. Her most valuable resource without exception and the one that lies at the core of this exhibition is the people of the state. For it is they who encounter and appraise the native materials, who provide the genius to turn slate into ornament, wool into warmth, and everyday life into a shared expressive experience.

In a very real sense, this exhibition is Vermont's gift to herself, the pieces merely rearranged on someone else's shelf. It provides an enlightening opportunity for the state to display its many brilliant parts, for an even wider public to appreciate, thus completing for now an informative, beautiful and useful picture.

Elaine Eff
Baltimore, Maryland

Contents

Always in Season: Folk Art and Traditional Culture in Vermont

Folk Art and Traditional Culture in Vermont

For many years scholars have battled unsuccessfully over definitions of folk art, so perhaps I should take some heed from the old Vermont saying "Save your breath to cool your soup." But because we have selected a number of objects and called them "Vermont folk art," it seems appropriate to explain why these items were chosen. As a folklorist I take the view that folk art is an artistic expression of a particular traditional culture. Hence the art itself must be seen in terms of this culture.

In Vermont, despite the influx of newcomers and the booming tourist industry, a traditional way of life still exists. This older way of life is rural and tied closely to the seasons. Custom rather than innovation is the basis of this lifestyle and activities are carried on as they have been for generations. Sugar is still made in the spring because that's when the sap flows. "When the wind's in the west, the sap flows the best." Some of those who pick the largest cucumbers still plant them before daybreak on the first Sunday in June. Others watch to see that the maple leaf is as big as a deer mouse's ear before they plant their corn. Butchering continues to be done when the weather turns cold and often at the full of the moon, when it is thought the meat will keep better. Logs are still skidded out in the snow. Thus does seasonal rhythm flow throughout Vermont traditional life. However, there is an interdependency of individual on individual. The family is important; the tight knit community is important. Each person participates and the shared activities bind both family and community together.

As a state, Vermont is partially an arbitrary land unit, bounded on the west by Lake Champlain, on the east by the Connecticut River, north and south by political "fences." Settlers from southern New England found their way up the Connecticut River Valley or used Lake Champlain as a travel route. Once the state of Vermont was established with its boundaries, there were other spheres of influences that weighed upon it. The Indians had never been given to living a sedentary life. They followed the game, and after the game was gone, the resort trade, ranging from Canada over to the Adirondacks and Lake George, down the eastern shore of Lake Champlain, across Vermont, stopping at places like the Mansfield House, and on into New Hampshire and the White Mountains, sometimes traveling all the way to Maine.

While some came to farm the land, to hunt, or to quarry, the lumber woods provided a strong lure and created a tradition of their own. Men from Maine, New Hampshire and the Maritimes joined local Vermonters in logging camps. Their ranks were swelled by French Canadians, Swedes, Finns, and Russians, each of whom tended to modulate and add to the traditional woods culture.

Hence, while Vermont as a state has an identity, it also has spheres of influence which extend beyond its borders. The Canadian-American line is official and arbitrary, but it is no natural barrier and people crossed it freely. Sometimes they were not even sure where it was. I have heard of families who intended to settle in Canada, carved out their farms, and built their homesteads, only to find that they had settled in Vermont.

Maple Sugaring Scene
c. 1910
Unknown, Vermont
Wood
17" H x 42½" L
Loaned by the
Shelburne Museum
    Here is an elaborately carved sugaring diorama. Sugaring has always been one of the favorite seasonal occupations in Vermont. Originally this was displayed together with a number of other tableaux in a Vermont Country Store.

Braided Rug
c. 1945
Belle D. Robinson,
Williamstown, Vermont
Wool
80" L x 47" W
Loaned by Flossie Humphrey
    When Allen Eaton did his research on New England handicrafts in the 1940's, he termed Belle Robinson "one of the best-known makers of braided rugs in New England." (Eaton, fig. 45)

Baling Twine Mat
1980
Imelda Lepine,
Morrisville, Vermont
Baling twine
30" L x 23" W
Loaned by Imelda Lepine
    On a farm recycled baling twine is easy to come by. Mrs. Lepine braided the twine and then wove it into a very durable door mat.

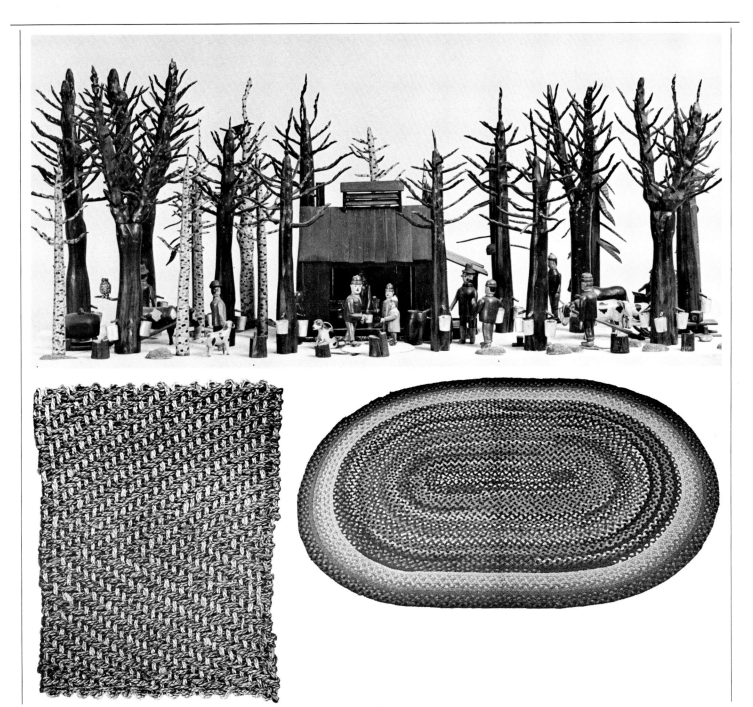

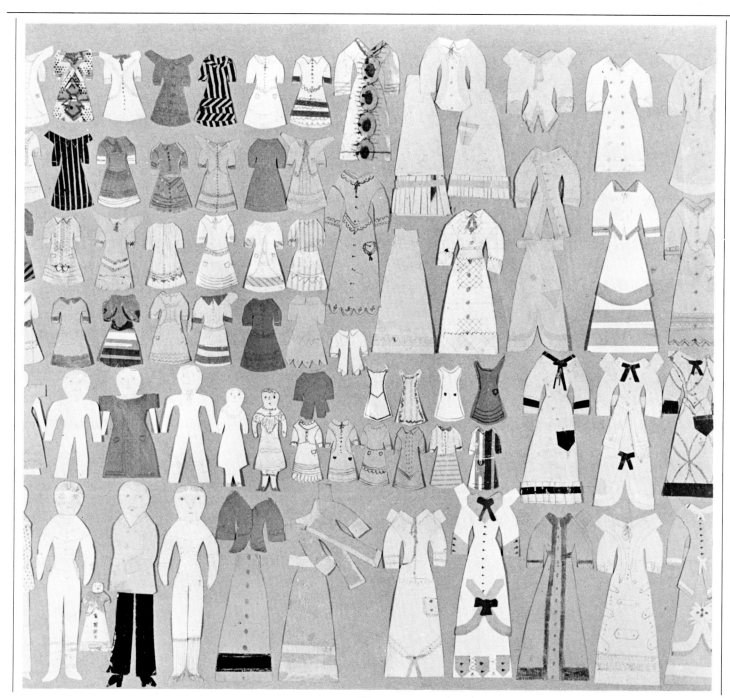

Paper Doll Picture
c. 1874-75
Nellie Britell,
Weybridge, Vermont
Cut paper
19¾" L x 17½" W
Loaned by the
Sheldon Museum

These paper dolls were made from writing paper, brown paper, bits of an old circus ad, anything that would serve. As a child, Mrs. Britell used to play with this household of paper dolls, dressing and undressing them in different outfits. If one lost an arm or a leg, a new one was cut out and pasted on with homemade glue of wheat flour and water. In later years when Nellie no longer cared to play with these dolls, she brought them out of their box and made this arrangement for posterity.

Baskets
c. 1956
Anonymous, Rutland, Vermont
Willow
15" H x 17" L x 15" W
12" H x 14" L x 12" W
Private collection

The maker of this basket emigrated from Poland in 1908 when he was fifteen and came to Florence, Vermont where he learned his life-long trade — that of a marble polisher. His daughter remembers her father going down to the swamp to gather willow to make his baskets. He apparently brought this knowledge with him from Poland and when he had the time would make various size baskets for his own and family use.

Basket
c. 1945
Lucas Nemkovich,
Springfield, Vermont
Willow and basswood
15" H x 17" L x 15½" W
Loaned by Michael Nemkovich

Lucas Nemkovich was born in Minsk, USSR, and came to Springfield, Vermont in 1902 to work in the Shoddy Mill. He made baskets as he remembered they had been made in his home country.

A number of ethnic groups have made their presence felt in Vermont, often appropriating areas of activity to themselves. For example, the French Canadians came as farmers, as loggers and later to work in the textile mills. Finns, Spaniards and a substantial number of northern Italians and Scots arrived to quarry granite, while southern Italians came to quarry marble. The Welsh emigrated from northern Wales to work in the slate quarries, and the Russians and Poles came to work in the mills around Springfield and West Rutland. However, few of these groups have had any lasting effect on Vermont's folk art despite the fact that they brought with them their own artistic heritage. There are a number of reasons for this. First was the desire of the first generation immigrants to "Americanize" their children. Some would not allow their offspring to speak anything but English in the home. Schools quickly assimilated the foreigners. Almost always the incentive was to conform to Vermont ways — "to be accepted."

We cannot totally overlook subtle influences originating in ethnic heritage — color choices, as in the bright use of colors by the French-Canadians, techniques, such as chip carving and fan whittling, even religious influences — but overall what has resulted is a folk art shaped by a Vermont environment and indicative of Vermont activities. A Swedish family might come to the state to work in a Proctor marble company, but a son, born in West Rutland and a marble setter all his life, makes miniature log cabins and houses out of chips of marble. These miniatures are built in the style of Vermont rather than Sweden. Thus it is the materials and the subject matter which help define Vermont folk art.

Vermonters who follow a traditional lifestyle, one that is by nature rural and generally determined by the natural environment, tend to use materials that come readily to hand for their art. These are both inexpensive and easily available. In many cases they are "recycled" materials, for Vermonters very definitely believe in the adage "waste not, want not" and art has never been a primary source of income. Coverlets are made from grain bags, bleached white and embroidered, rugs are braided or hooked over burlap from the remains of clothing so well worn that it can no longer be remade for a younger child, dolls are constructed from paper, corn husks, apples, clothespins, even a goose's wishbone, and dressed from "scrounges."

Fungus, wood, slate, marble, soapstone and granite are all easy to come by and have been used in various artistic creations. These creations almost always have a functional or symbolic use as well as an artistic value. At one end of the spectrum stands the old pump in the dooryard with a decorative design hand-painted on four sides or the old hay fork with black and red bands painted around it, not only so that it might be quickly identified by the owner, but because "it just looked good."

At the other end of the scale, objects might have no function at all but be an attempt to represent something in diminutive form. An example is the miniature snow roller that Ed Cowdry made because he wanted to recreate one from memory. As he told me "when you start from nothing, just from memory — no patterns, nothing — you got to do a lot of figuring. When I finished," he continued, "I took it over to Clyde Hastings 'cause he'd rolled the roads for quite a while. He looked it all over and said 'That's pretty near perfect. That's what I call art'."

This comment is significant because it implies a number of things about folk art. First, it suggests the relationships of the object to traditional learning; the maker thinks through how a snow roller is made, with meticulous attention to detail, down to the correct type of harness for the six-horse team. It also indicates the object's basis in shared experience, unlike the characteristically individual vision of fine art. Finally, it contains an aesthetic understood by both maker and viewer: "That's pretty near perfect. That's what I call art."

Folk art is rooted in shared activities of the local community. These activities are not only shared by family and friends, but they help shape the individual's point of view, a viewpoint that is based on the reality of personal experience and communal activity rather than creation in isolation. The folk artist expresses this reality in concrete terms rather than in abstractions. For the traditional artist, creation has a purpose. When Henry Palmer makes a duck decoy, he wants to make it look as near to a live duck as possible. He says, "I fooled a person, I fooled a duck, but I won't rest until I can fool a fox." Those who hunt with Henry share his practical view of a good decoy and admire his workmanship.

In his later years, after his trapping days were finished, Ernest Hooker whittled a replica of a steel trap from a pine log. His associates marveled at his skill in whittling the chain, spring, and giant jaws of the trap, but they wondered even more because the replica worked just like the steel trap did. Today a handful of these traps are still around, treasured by men who are hunters and trappers themselves. Some actually knew the old bear trapper, which enhanced the trap's value to them. Others had only heard of him, admired his work and shared his knowledge of the woods. When a city person looks at the trap and is told that it "really works" he is not usually struck by the workmanship or how it was made. He wants to know "how such a thing can hold a bear!"

Whittled Bear Trap
c. 1950
Ernest C. Hooker,
Forest Dale, Vermont
Pine
36" L x 8" W, chain 36"
Loaned by
Mrs. Raymond Gerow

Mr. Hooker was both a carpenter and a trapper. He trapped forty-five bears throughout his lifetime, selling them live to zoos and circuses as well as to a restaurant outside Middlebury known as "The Bear." It was after he had given up both his carpentry and trapping that he began to whittle bear traps, replicas of the steel ones he had once used. Towards the end of his life, he made a handful of these, still treasured by the few family members and friends who were the lucky recipients of his handiwork.

Applehead Doll

c. 1890
Probably Kate Dewey Squires,
Montpelier, Vermont
Apple, clothespin, fabric
7½" L
Loaned by the Vermont
Historical Society

Another common type of
doll made from household
materials. A new head has been
made by Gussie Levarn of
Bristol, Vermont, since
appleheads seldom survive
mice and aging very well.

Goose Wishbone Doll

19th century
Artist unknown,
Windsor, Vermont
Goose wishbone, cotton
5" L x 4" W
Loaned by the Vermont
Historical Society

This doll is typical of many
made on the farm using the
wishbone of one of the barnyard
geese (the down and feathers
were saved for pillows and
mattresses, the wings for
dusters) and remnants of white
cotton were embroidered to
give a loving touch.

Drake and Hen Broadbill Decoys

c. 1955
Gerald Tremblay,
Alburg Springs, Vermont
Pine, painted
12½" L x 7½" H x 5½" W
Loaned by the Vermont
Historical Society

As a child Gerald Tremblay
was stricken with polio, leaving
his legs useless. When he was
seventeen he began carving —
first whittling a pencil, then a
decoy. It took him ten years to
perfect his technique and the
realistic painting of his decoys
but as he improved, his fame
grew. He began by selling his
decoys for $1.50 because if he
charged more, his local clientele
around Alburg Springs "would
go out and buy plastic decoys."
Although he made over 8,000
decoys, it is almost impossible
to buy one today. Besides
decoys, he carved replicas of
local birds like woodcock,
bluejays, grosbeaks and
cardinals.

Miniature House
c. 1915
William J. Morrison,
Waterford, Vermont
Wood
35½″ H x 39¼″ W x 30″ D
Loaned by the Fairbanks
Museum and Planetarium

After being crippled by polio, William Morrison did a great deal of woodworking, making everything from rolling pins to crokinole games, fine cabinet work, and miniatures. Among his best work were his miniatures, which show a great attention to detail. He built a church that was a replica (except for one level of the steeple) of that in his home town of Waterford, and a miniature house about which he said "If I was building a house for myself, that's how I'd built it." His rooms left nothing to the imagination. There was even soap in the dish over the bathtub. For some of the furnishings and the clothing for his people, he enlisted the aid of his daughter.

Miniature Blacksmith Shop
c. 1911
William J. Morrison,
Waterford, Vermont
Wood, iron
15″ H x 13¼″ W x 10¼″ D
Loaned by the Fairbanks
Museum and Planetarium

William J. Morrison was a blacksmith when he was paralyzed by polio at the age of forty-one. He didn't have enough strength to move his left hand but he would use it as a vise to hold a piece of wood and then work on it with his right hand. One of the first things he did to help regain his strength was to build a miniature blacksmith shop. This was complete with tools, forge, and a pair of horses waiting to be shod. Apparently he could take a piece of wood, draw a pattern on it and then with a stiff backed saw and a half round file, shape it "so you'd think it came out of a turning lathe. But he'd made it all by hand. He had the eye and it came natural for him to do things like that." (Arthur Morrison)

Miniature Church
c. 1963
Euclide and Delia Giroux,
St. Albans, Vermont
Wood
28½" H x 15½" W x 21" D
Loaned by the Franklin County
Museum and
Mrs. Annette Richards

Euclide Giroux enjoyed making things with his jack knife and decided, as he had two cousins who were priests, to build a miniature church. He and his wife, Delia, went about the task in leisure fashion, taking about two years to complete the church, not satisfied until every detail was finished. Sometimes Giroux would make the same item three or four times before it was right. His wife made the windows and the furnishings and added a realistic touch by cutting a favorite priest's name out of an old **Bulletin** and glueing it above the confessional. Giroux electrified the church and it was always lit when visitors came to the house.

Although folk art is rooted in shared activities, it is still intensely personal for the artist. It is because traditional life is shared so completely by family and neighbors — because each individual depends on and is important to everyone in the community, that what the folk artist produces is just as meaningful, just as significant to any member of that community. Frequently it is a means by which the artist participates in local life. Gerald Tremblay was stricken with polio as a young child, leaving him unable to work like his brother. When he was eighteen, he turned to carving, mostly decoys at first, because he lived near the lake and almost everyone around hunted ducks on Lake Champlain. His decoys were soon in demand and he became known as the finest carver around.

William Morrison was a blacksmith until he was forty-one years old, when he too contracted polio and was paralyzed. One of his first projects as he tried to regain strength in his arms was to build a miniature blacksmith shop, complete with all the tools, the same tools that during his early years as a blacksmith he had made for himself. Polio had cursed and blessed Morrison with the time to create. Through the creation of his miniature blacksmith shop, Morrison was once more living the way of life he knew so well.

Although Ken Beane had always made things for his children as they were growing up, "so that we could see what they looked like — because we had no pictures of them and he wanted us to see how they went," it wasn't until his health failed that he began to make his miniatures in earnest. His daughter explains, "He wanted something to do because he couldn't get out. He couldn't race his horses any more and he couldn't do things like that, so he wanted something to do with his hands." His miniatures reflected his trade as a harness maker and his lifelong interest in horses.

Like Beane, when Burleigh Woodard became too old and ill to work in the woods with his team, he turned to making scale miniatures with his jack knife out of scraps of wood from his brother's sawmill. He made teams, harnessed with shoelaces and decorated with turned copper wire, pulling wagons and snow rollers. Through his teams, Woodard continued to live and work in the woods long after he had lost the health or strength to do so. Further, his creations could be admired by those who had shared that way of life with him. Through his artistry, he became the spokesman for it.

It is not uncommon to find an individual turning to his creative abilities and making things when mishap and injury strike. It is as if his artistic spirit is allowed the time to flower in a way that is not always possible in a life of continuous seasonal activity. Now through his art he once more participates in community life, becomes a visual spokesman for it, and relieves his own isolation.

By far the most common feature in Vermont's folk art is its narrative impulse. Paintings, carvings, quilts, hooked rugs, and miniatures all seem to tell a story of how it was, embodying a personal view of the past. Sometimes corroborative material has provided the background to understand a work of folk art in its context, as in a letter from Mrs. Grant describing twenty blocks of her remembrance quilt, a quilt that took her seven years to complete and won her first prize at the Tunbridge World Fair in 1946. Her comments give outsiders a rare understanding of the narrative and personal nature of much of folk art. "My son's registered redbone fox hound. I drawed her picture as she lay in front of the syringa bush in the front yard. A natural hunter and a great pet." Or "My full-blooded jersey cow. Her name is Susan. She gave rich milk, and I have made delicious yellow butter and cottage cheese from it."

Farm and Home Memories Quilt
1939-1946
Ina Grant, Chelsea, Vermont
Muslin, single strand
embroidered blocks, pieced
with colored four-point stars
70" L x 72" W
Private collection

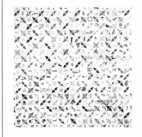

Mrs. Ina Grant
1881-1975

Mrs. Ina Hackett Grant was born on a farm in Chelsea in 1881. And, as her daughter-in-law says, "the farm was where her heart was." Because her husband was a rural mail carrier in the days of horses and snow rollers, they moved off their farm down into the village, but they always returned after the mail route was done to help cut wood or do other chores. Sometimes Mrs. Grant would walk the five miles to the farm and every summer she worked in the hayfield. But she was a woman of many talents, a poet and an artist in her fancy work of crocheting, quilting and rugmaking. One of her finest pieces is her "Memory Quilt" which took her seven years to make and had the honor of taking first prize at the 1946 Tunbridge World's Fair.

The quilt is entirely stitched by hand to a homespun blanket made by Mrs. Grant's mother and to a backing of white muslin. The decorated blocks, one hundred seventy-two in all, are embroidered with one thread of six-strand cotton on pieces of white octagonal muslin, four and one-half inches in diameter. All the blocks preserve some special memory of her life. In a letter to Allen Eaton, Mrs. Grant described twenty of the most important blocks; her comments are included here because of the insight such statements give into the creation of folk art.

1. Wood-colored house and barn, at upper right, where I lived eight years. My oldest son was born here.
2. White house, with pine trees in front is where I live now. My youngest son was born here.
3. Wood-colored farm house, at lower left, with syringa bush and lilac bush in front yard. My husband was born here. I lived here about nine years. This is where I drawed so many of my pictures.
4. Little farm house, wood-color, at lower right, my childhood home.
5. Sugar house with sap buckets hanging on trees, where we made such good Vermont maple sugar.
6. Yoke of oxen with man drawing sugar wood.
7. Pair of white horses and man plowing. Getting ready in the spring for planting.
8. Pair [of] white horses with load of hay, with rake left beside it, my son's team on his home farm.
9. The couple dancing certainly is one of my favorites, as I like to dance. They look as though it comes natural to them, and they seem to be enjoying it.
10. My Christmas cactus, sometimes there is around sixty buds and blossoms on it at one time, and are such a beautiful shade of pink. It is around twenty-five years old.
11. The man with gun and two hunting dogs in partridge hunting time. Note the beautiful tree with autumn leaves in the background.
12. My son's registered redbone fox hound. I drawed her picture as she lay in front of the syringa bush in the front yard. A natural hunter and a great pet.
13. My full-blooded jersey cow, at lower left, her name is Susan, she gave very rich milk, and I have made delicious yellow butter and cottage cheese from it.
14. At extreme right, my hen house and yard with hens in yard as it looked from my kitchen window.
15. Bouquet of wild flowers, near center of quilt, I picked them, ten varieties beside the road between the two houses, and put them together in bouquet, and embroidered in natural colors. The houses were about 25 rods apart.
16. The bull at right of quilt is one of our neighbors. It is a registered Brown Swiss, 6 months old.
17. The little white driving horse, with string bells, and the couple in the old red sleigh, makes me think of "Old Times" when I used to go sleigh riding.
18. My blue slate turkeys out among the corn and pumpkins.
19. Two race horses at the World's Fair at Tunbridge, Vermont. I always enjoy the horse racing at the Fair as I like horses.
20. The United States Flag, for "Victory." ●

Often such corroborative evidence is retained in families. Mae Chandler's stair runner is so treasured by her grandchildren that they have divided it amongst themselves. All can explain the significance of the various pieces, for each riser represented a different family member's interest, or perhaps a scene that was significant in the life of the family: the homestead, a favorite pet, sugaring with a faithful team of oxen, deer hunting. These scenes, with their personal significance, embody a series of memories shared by the family. Thus a rug can evoke a whole history to the family that understands it. The images are a series of visual clues to past events.

Sometimes when a piece of folk art is no longer preserved in the family or by those who understood the context, it is difficult to reconstruct the story it tells. Today the specific significance of these scenes may well be forgotten, but the art remains to give us clues, if only we could understand them. A good example is the depiction of a disreputable looking young man on a Bennington stoneware jug and the inscription "In for ten years or Billy McGue's crime." When this was first made, Billy McGue's crime must have been a major local event known by all. A more personal item was made in 1847 by S. Merrill, a farmer in Peacham. Like Mrs. Grant, he recorded family life on the farm by carving scenes on a powder horn. Unlike Mrs. Grant, he didn't leave a written account spelling out their significance.

Folk paintings most frequently tell a story. Some may carefully encapsulate a familiar scene; others are a composite of remembered activities. Bessie Drennan frequently would paint childhood memories with variations that suited her fancy. If she painted a June wedding with autumn leaves in the background, she didn't worry about inconsistency. The houses, the church, the people and their activities were all part of her life.

Stair Runner
1958
Mae Chandler,
Taftsville, Vermont
Wool, burlap
91½" L x 25" W
Loaned by Marilyn Ware
and Edward S. Whitney

For some time Mae Chandler had been thinking about making a stair runner. Three months before Christmas she decided that if she was going to do it, she better do it while she was alive and that she would make it for her daughter. Her sisters helped her draw some of the designs that would be meaningful to her daughter and husband: the house they lived in, a favorite dog, Joe, familiar landmarks like the covered bridge and the church in Taftsville, and things they liked to do such as sugaring and deer hunting. She had fourteen "pictures" in all and when she was finished, she went over and laid it and then invited her daughter in. "She was flabbergasted."

Jug, "Billy McGue's Crime"
c. 1861-1881
E. and L. P. Norton,
Bennington, Vermont
Stoneware, cobalt blue
7" H x 8¼" Diam.
Loaned by the
Bennington Museum

Decorations representing human figures are seldom found on stoneware, however, there are several Bennington jugs with inscriptions commemorating unusual events. Obviously at one time Billy McGue's crime was well known.

Marion Hastings also paints largely from memory. She may put in an extra house or widen a stream, but her paintings are of activities she remembers: rolling the roads, skating parties, sugaring, or a herd of cows crossing a brook. Lee Hull has an explanation that goes with most of his paintings. One of his favorites is of a camp in Swanton where he and his family went every fall for almost forty years to gather berries and balsam for the Christmas wreaths they made. Finally the year came when they didn't go. He felt so badly about it that he painted a picture of how it used to be. The painting tells it all. There is Blackie, the dog who used to attach himself to the Hulls for the two weeks that they were at camp; "the boy from Windsor cutting wood;" Reggie fishing; Lena, in front of the camp; and an old timer, Ned Daniels, "who didn't care what the weather or the going was," with Mrs. Hull in the canoe while Lee holds it. Once again, through the painting, the Hulls were back at camp reliving those times and participating once more in familiar activities.

Roland Rochette who says "I'm not a painter — I make collages" has a story for all of his pictures. "I like to do things that the younger generation haven't seen. I think it's kind of instructive for the younger people. Younger people, a lot of them, don't believe what the older people did and how hard they worked." His subject matter follows his life, from working for the Canadian-Pacific Railroad to logging and farming. Again, his stories are about the activities going on in his collages.

These "narrative paintings" fall well within the definition of folk art that has been established for the context of this exhibition. They reflect a traditional lifestyle and a shared community experience and aesthetic which is at the same time a personal expression within a traditional mode.

In the same way quilts, rugs or paintings might tell a story, miniatures or carvings also recreate the maker's way of life. Frequently miniatures are replicas of individual buildings. For example, the "Thornton" bird house was made by Bob Thornton as a model of his home. Miniature villages reveal the maker's conception of a Vermont town; they have Vermont churches, houses, barns and sawmills. Sometimes the miniatures are worked on by more than one member of the family, making it a joint effort, a sociable activity. William Morrison, when asked about his miniature house would answer, "If I was building a house for myself, that's how I'd build it." His daughter helped him with some of the accessories and dressing the people. In the same way, Mr. and Mrs. Euclide Giroux teamed up on their miniature church. Mr. Giroux made the building from "odds and ends" using a coping saw and a jack knife. His wife provided the furnishings. A mother and her eleven year old daughter made a miniature replica of the town of Montgomery.

Winter Scene
1979
Marion Hastings,
West Windsor, Vermont
Hardboard, oils
22¼" L x 18½" H
Loaned by Jane Beck

It was Lee Hull who first encouraged Marion Hastings to take up the brush. She paints mostly from memory and her scenes are usually full of activity. Perhaps she will add a house or two or widen a brook, but mostly her scenes reflect West Windsor as she knew it.

Bird House
c. 1940
Bob Thornton,
Richford, Vermont
Wood
18" H x 18" W x 17½" D
Loaned by Joe Duggan

This is a replica of Thornton's own house, known as an "outstanding landmark" in the town of Richford.

"The Old Kitchen"
c. 1955
Bessie Drennan,
Woodbury, Vermont
Oil on canvas board
24" H x 20" W
Courtesy of
Mrs. Stephen Greene

When Bessie Drennan (1882-1961) was about seventy she wanted somebody to paint a picture of the old family place where she and her sisters lived. When she had no luck at finding anyone, she attended an adult education course in Montpelier and in one evening learned all she felt she needed to know about painting. She then went and did the job herself— and began her painting career.

Usually filled with scenes of activity, her paintings are composites of nostalgic remembrances from her childhood.

31.

Miniature Village
1877
Mary P. Anderson and
Elvina Anderson,
Montgomery, Vermont
Wood, glass, paper
8″ H x 10½″ W x 10½″ D
Loaned by the Franklin
County Museum

This miniature village,
said to be based on Mont-
gomery, was handmade by a
mother and daughter when the
daughter was eleven years
of age.

The Parting
c. 1920
Frank W. Moran,
Bakersfield, Vermont
Mahogany
9½" H x 5 x 5
Private collection
    When he could get it,
Moran liked to use mahogany
because it is a cross-grained
wood and he didn't have to
worry about it checking.

Cane
c. 1917
Frank Moran,
Bakersfield, Vermont
Wood
34¼" L x 1¼" W Head: 4⅝"
Loaned by Pruella Gibson
    A cane Moran carved for his
father's use in his old age.

Carvings also frequently tell a story. One of Vermont's most prolific carvers was Frank Moran. He was a carpenter by trade, often decorating his furniture with his carvings. He used decorative motifs as well as symbolic carvings. On a gunstock he might carve a bear and a beaver or a deer and squirrel — representative of something he might hunt. He spent a great deal of time in the woods and depended on game for his meat supply. There is a well known local story about Frank shooting bear. The most exciting version is that Moran was picking berries when he suddenly turned to find himself facing a large bear. He grabbed his gun, loaded with bird shot, and fired one shot, killing the bear. Next a cub appeared which he killed with a second shot. Just as he was heaving a sigh of relief, a third bear appeared in hot pursuit and he killed this creature with his third and last shot. Others with a more conservative viewpoint claim that he only killed one bear or, at most, a she-bear and cub.

    Moran's carvings sometimes depicted whole scenes. One of these was of the elusive Vermont "painter" (panther) crouching behind a log waiting to pounce upon a deer which had come down to drink from the brook. The carver was familiar with panthers in the East Fairfield area and could demonstrate its cry "like a woman screaming" as distinguished from the howl of a bobcat. Apparently, Moran rejected this piece as not good enough to put on a dower chest. However, another chest which he carved for the niece of a close friend depicts the farm that the family worked: the house, the barn, even the garage, which Moran himself had built.

Weathervanes and signs were often concrete representations of the important concerns of the makers or proprietors. A Merino ram proclaims the former pride of a farm, which in later years has gone from raising sheep to raising cows. A train weathervane was made by Cyrus Curtis as a symbol of his lifelong work on the railroad; a sheepshead (fish) by Cecil Benton depicts one he caught. He took the exact outline of the fish and from that carved his weathervane.

Trade signs, handmade within the community, can also be considered folk art. A good example of this is Amideé Thibault's bicycle sign. Thibault was a jack-of-all-trades who ran a bicycle and carriage repair shop. Both a wheelwright and a talented carver, he made, in 1895, a trade sign for his business which showed a wooden figure atop a high wheel bicycle. This he placed on the roof of his "Bicycle, Livery and Carriage Shop" and attracted both local people and outsiders who could see the sign from the train on the way to St. Albans.

Hand in hand with the narrative and representational aspect of Vermont folk art comes the patriotic impulse as in carvings of famous Americans like Washington and Lincoln, a Paul Revere doll, or the depiction of a major political event of the day. The campaign of Benjamin Harrison and John Tyler was immortalized on the Fairfax stoneware jug, the Civil War by the G.A.R. hooked rug, or certain presidents celebrated, as in the embroidered likeness of John Quincy Adams and the Windsor County rug commemorating Vermont's native son, Calvin Coolidge.

It is interesting to note in this exhibition that almost all the objects show a reflection of the past and the present. The future and the world of fantasy seldom seem to be the subject of the Vermont folk artist.

Fish Weathervane
c. 1936
Cecil R. Benton,
Vergennes , Vermont
Wood
11" H x 22" L
Loaned by Bill Benton

Cecil R. Benton caught a very large sheepshead fish. To memorialize it, he traced around it with pencil to make a template and then carved his vane.

Paul Revere Doll
1940
Christena Foster,
Stowe, Vermont
Pine, fabric
17½" H x 9½" W x 2½" D
Loaned by
Mrs. Bessie Foster Harlow

Mrs. Foster was a great whittler, a pastime that she seemed to have picked up from her father. She began to carve dolls out of pine and bass wood in 1939, and before she died she had made over three hundred. Her daughter explained that after making some colonial ladies and Indian dolls, Mrs. Foster wanted to make an historical character and decided on Paul Revere. "She dressed him and made all those tiny buttonholes and painted the old shoe buttons over with gold for his buttons on his coat. He's got a vest, he's got a shirt with tiny buttonholes, he's got a necktie and he's got a hat."

Jug
c. 1840
Lewis Cady, Fairfax, Vermont
Stoneware, cobalt blue
16¾" H x 9" Diam.
Loaned by Duane E. Merrill

This jug is interesting because of its painted blue cobalt cartoon, "old Tip" in a canoe, which represented the 1840 presidential campaign slogan of William Henry Harrison and John Tyler: "Tippecanoe and Tyler too."

Train Weathervane
Before 1900
Cyrus Curtis, Bradford, Vermont
Oxidized copper
42¼" H x 31" L
Loaned by
Mrs. Charlotte T. Blodgett

Cyrus Curtis worked on the railroad most of his life as an engineer. When he retired he made this weathervane to put on his stable roof.

G.A. R. Hooked Rug
c. 1860
Artist unknown, Vermont
cotton and wool, burlap backing
36" L x 21" W
Loaned by the Vermont
Historical Society

An example of a rug made by a mother, wife or sweetheart for the absent loved one who was in the 24th Army Corps of the 9th Regiment of Riflemen, 2nd Squadron, 2nd Platoon.

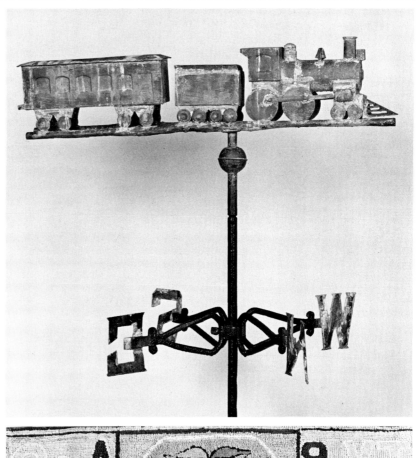

Another form of Vermont folk art is the "love token," something made for the absent wife or sweetheart. This form was common among seamen and lumbermen, men who shared occupations which removed them from their homes for long periods. By far the most common far away occupation for Vermonters was logging, although this exhibit indicates that Vermonters also spent time at sea.

In such occupations, men rubbed shoulders with others from different backgrounds. They shared a way of life and learned from each other. In logging camps their free time was in the evening when they sang, told stories, and carved gifts for those at home. The lumber camps appear to be one of the major sources for introducing "tramp art" into Vermont. Tramp art flourished in the late nineteenth and early twentieth century and is thought to have developed from the European tradition of chipcarving, a technique of notching or gouging wood in a v-shaped design.

It makes sense that Vermonters were exposed to techniques of chip carving, whittled fans and a type of work called "crown of thorns" (where numerous pieces of wood were notched together in an interlocking and overlapping fashion and layered to have a three-dimensional look) in the logging camps. This is not to say that all tramp art in Vermont came from the logging camps (another good source would have been the men working on the railroad) but it does suggest that these camps were one important origin for these particular techniques. During the long winter evenings different carving and whittling styles were positive virtues and shared freely.

Finns, Russians and Swedes swelled the population of these camps and, the influences of these ethnic groups are easily traced. Spruce gum boxes, hollowed out to hold a present of spruce gum and often decorated with some form of chip carving were frequently made for wives or girlfriends. Cedar fans whittled from one piece of cedar, a typically Scandinavian technique, were also popular items. Chester Nutting's grandfather learned this style of carving in the lumber camps and taught his grandson. Chet made his own variation on this type of carving by whittling birds instead of fans. In later life he taught this to another young man, who today makes his living whittling cedar birds with fan tails and thus continues the tradition.

We know that in at least one case, the Crown of Thorns technique was learned by a Vermonter from a Russian as they shared life in a lumber camp. This Vermonter made a picture frame for his wife out of interlocking pieces of cedar. Others used this same technique to make even more elaborate structures, as in a model of a logging camp boarding house, an example which also expressed the same narrative impulse mentioned earlier.

Another element in Vermont folk art that must be considered is the use of a pattern or decorative design as in the old pump or the chest with a handpainted geometric motif. Generally these appear on objects whose function clearly outweighs the decorative significance. Furniture and baskets are good examples since a chest is used for storage, a basket as a necessary container. It might also be pointed out that on the latter, geometric designs are much easier to weave than is a scene, which would almost have to be painted on.

Hooked Rug
c. 1920
Artist unknown, probably Windsor County, Vermont
Wool and cotton over burlap
60½" L x 38" W
Loaned by
Mrs. Barbara Chiolino

This rug reflects the great local pride that Vermonters felt for native son Calvin Coolidge. All the towns of Windsor County are included and marked with the first initial of the name.

Embroidered Portrait
c. 1830
Zeruah Higley Guernsey,
Castleton, Vermont
Linen, silk
9⅛″ H x 6⅜″ W
Loaned by the
Castleton Historical Society

Patriotic sentiment seems to play a part in folk art. Here Zeruah Guernsey has embroidered a portrait of John Quincy Adams, probably about the time he was president, and therefore this effort would predate her famous carpet.

37.

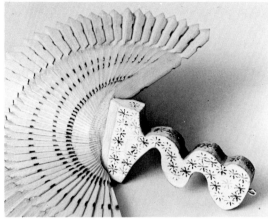

Fan
c. 1972
Chester Nutting
West Danville, Vermont
Cedar
6″ H x 8″ W x 3″ D
Loaned by Edmond Menard
   This is a typical example of a fan whittled out of one piece of cedar. Except for the wood-burning, this is probably identical to those Nutting's grandfather learned to carve in a logging camp.

Pelican with Fish
1978
Edmond Menard,
Marshfield, Vermont
Cedar
6″ H x 6″ W
Loaned by Jane Beck
   This pelican with a fish is identical to those pelicans Chester Nutting used to carve. The fish is carved separately and held in the pelican's bill by a small pin.

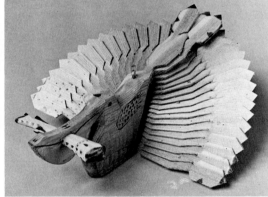

Fan-Tailed Cedar Bird
c. 1970
Chester Nutting,
West Danville, Vermont
Cedar
6″ H x 6″ W
Loaned by Edmond Menard
   This is Chester Nutting's characteristic bird that earned him the name of "Bird Man."

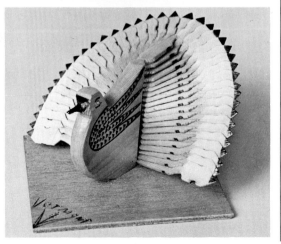

38.

Bird Sign
1980
Edmond Menard,
Marshfield, Vermont
Cedar
12" H x 26" W
Loaned by Edmond Menard

This sign is a good example of a modern trade sign that can be considered folk art. Edmond has carved it by hand and set it high atop a pole to beckon those looking for novelty and crafts along Route 2.

From Generation to Generation

One of the most prolific whittlers in Vermont was Chester Nutting of West Danville. He learned how to whittle cedar fans from his grandfather, a technique he had picked up in the logging camps. From the time he was a child, Chet was always whittling and one day as he was working on a fan, he produced his first bird — something that he was to become well known for, and something which gave him the title of "Bird Man" in later life. For thirty-three years, he worked as a carpenter and it wasn't until 1965 when he broke his leg that he began whittling in earnest — at first to make Christmas presents and then, as the popularity of his birds grew, to fill orders. As he said, "I don't know if I'd ever kept it up again if it hadn't been for breaking my leg." In 1967, the local radio station invited Nutting to be interviewed and as a result of that program, he began to get orders from as far away as Olympia, Washington. By the time of his death, he had whittled over 50,000 birds.

In his later years it is said that Chester Nutting desperately hoped that one of his own grandsons might follow in his footsteps, but none seemed so inclined. Then in 1974, he happened to be driving on a back road in Cabot when he experienced car trouble. He pulled into the nearest farm and a young man came out to assist him. It proved a fateful meeting for both men. They knew each other for only six months, but in those few months Chester Nutting taught Edmond Menard his art of whittling birds — right from the selection of a female cedar tree, to preserving it (Nutting used to bury his boards under the snow or preserve them in the refrigerator while Menard uses a freezer) to the finished product of whittled birds and wood-burned markings.

Today Edmond is known as "Bird Man II" and continues Nutting's whittling tradition. He even works from Nutting's old work bench, using some of the same knives honed to a fine edge with a leather strop, and clamping the bird's tail feathers with a set of his mentor's clamps.

For the past four years, Edmond has been able to support himself by figuring out how many birds he must sell to live in the manner he wishes. During the winter months, he sets about carving these birds, making a certain number every week. During the summer and fall months, tourists beat a path to his door. He also used to exhibit at craft shows, but since **Yankee Magazine** (June 1980, pp. 164-165) did an article on him, he has all the orders he can fill. ●

It must also be remembered that folk art patterns frequently mean something to both the artists and their local community. For example, a "Log Cabin" quilt asserts the importance of hearth and home and sunshine and shadows, or in a variation of the "Log Cabin" known as the "Barn Raising" the title refers to how the quilt would be put together, by building up into the center as was done in an actual barn raising. A practical consideration was that these patterns lent themselves to incorporating a great variety of old materials.

Native American designs were also full of symbolic meaning shared by whole tribes. Among the Abenaki a popular pattern was ⟋⟍ or in a more linear context: ⟍⟋. This design signified the power of the plant world with all its spiritual, medicinal and life-giving properties, although to the uninitiated this appears simply as a pleasing decorative design. In many cases the significance of these designs has long been forgotten, for they hold no importance for a people who do not share the tribe's beliefs and rituals.

The major part of this discussion has been on what Vermont folk art is, but equally important questions are who treasures this folk art? Is it still in the communities where it was done? Or has it found a wider audience? And what, if anything, can be determined about the aesthetics of folk art?

The point has already been made that folk art is rooted in shared activities of family, neighbors, fellow workers. Historically, the artist's creation remains in the family and community where it was made. Local attitudes about the folk artist usually combine pride and emotional attachment: pride in the individual's workmanship, emotional attachment based upon a long standing and personal relationship. In some cases an individual's work never leaves the family circle. A mother makes a quilt for each of her five children or a grandfather carefully hand-carves and crafts muskets for each of his grandsons. These pieces take a great deal of time and effort. They are truly a labor of love and will be treasured by each recipient. Sometimes close friends and neighbors will be honored with such a gift. Locally, the object is admired and often the topic of conversation.

For example, in Fairlee people talk about Jim Whitcomb's clock. He had spent most of his life in Post Mills and in his spare time used to make clocks. His neighbors still remember one above all others.

"He made it in 1935. He made the whole thing himself — the wooden works, the gears — the pendulum is lead gilded. He made the dolls, he made the face, he drew the numbers and everything. And in the little cubbyhold beneath the face, he placed a fireplace with a shotgun hanging over the mantel. And in one chair he has a man in a black suit and high black shoes. The little lady sits in a rocking chair and when the pendulum sways, she rocks. He made the chairs, he made the dolls, he made the clothes, every stitch of them himself. and when it first came out everybody was crazy about it. Everybody came to see it and admire it."

Fifty years later it is still remembered and treasured by a family member but as she says "It's too bad it isn't where people can see it." Here is an item that has transcended the community. Moreover, fifty years later, when few people remember Jim Whitcomb, the clock stands on its own as something people beyond the community consider a marvel.

Because there was never extra time in the traditional workaday world, a folk artist usually did not have the opportunity to be prolific in his artistry. A woman might set her mind to making her daughter a stair rug for Christmas or a father might make his son a traverse sled, but these are often one of a kind items. It is not until the folk artist has time, due to retirement, sickness, or injury, that he is able to create more abundantly and perhaps gain a reputation as an artist in the community.

Chester Nutting, known as "Bird Man," would probably never have whittled his 50,000 birds, if he hadn't broken his leg. First he turned to whittling to make Christmas presents. Then as demands grew he took orders.

In canvassing the state for folk art it was his birds and shelves that appeared most frequently, especially within a one hundred mile radius of Danville. Anyone who was interested in traditional art had a Chester Nutting bird. Most of these people knew Nutting personally and treasured his creations. But these birds found a wider audience as well for he took orders from all over the country.

Grandfather Clock
1935
Jim Whitcomb,
Post Mills, Vermont
Maple, butternut and cherry
83" H x 19½" W x 9½" D
Courtesy of
Mrs. William Fitzgerald

Jim Whitcomb spent most of his adult life working at the Rod and Gun Factory in Post Mills. In his spare time he used to make and repair clocks. This particular one he made all by hand and when he finished, it caused something of a sensation in the neighborhood. Almost fifty years later it is still remembered and widely admired.

Beaded Head Band
c. 1900
Artist unknown, Abenaki,
Pierreville, Quebec
Black worsted twill, beads
3¾" H x 26" Circum.
Loaned by the Museum of Man,
National Museums of Canada
Photograph courtesy of the
National Museums of Canada,
Neg. #81-15234

This is a shaped headband of black worsted twill, the ends terminating in two points. The edges are bound with purple velvet, and the upper edge is trimmed with colored and clear beads. In the center there is a beaded quatrefoil, and on each side, a white stem with colored leaves. This design signified the power of the plant world with all its spiritual, medicinal and life-giving properties.

41.

When an artist works continuously in one area for a long period of time, most people who know him or are interested in traditional art have one of his pieces. Frank Moran, "the woodcarver of Little Egypt," is another example. He too had been a carpenter but he had carved all his life. When he turned seventy he stopped his carpentry and turned to full time carving in a little shop across from his farm house. He had no electricity and everything was done by hand. Although he died in 1967, he is well-remembered in the Bakersfield area. Old friends and neighbors still treasure pieces that he carved years ago. Moran was something of a local celebrity, famous for both his carving and his fiddling. Frequently, he had been known to turn down a high price for a piece of work and then give it to a friend or neighbor who he thought would appreciate it more. He was generous with his friends, often carving something for a person willing to supply the wood. But his neighbors also bought from him: canes, gunracks, carved gunstocks, chests, cupboards, mirrors, anything he carved.

Frank was a good Catholic as well as a fine carver and when the little stone church of St. Anthony's was built in 1940 in East Fairfield he supplied it with some of his finest carvings: the twelve stations of the cross, the crucifix, and the statue of St. Anthony with a child.

"Lost in the Desert"
c. 1930
Frank W. Moran,
Bakersfield, Vermont
Applewood
15¾" H x 11½" Diam.
Private collection
This was one of Moran's favorite pieces and one he did not want to part with. It is carved out of a solid block of applewood and is based on his own brief sojourn in the southwest.

St. Anthony
1940
Frank W. Moran,
Bakersfield, Vermont
Oak
26" H x 9½" W x 6½" D
Courtesy of the St. Anthony Catholic Church of East Fairfield

Frank W. Moran
1965
Photograph courtesy of The Artistic Alliance,
Betsy and Tom Melvin

Moran Chest
c. 1955
Frank W. Moran,
Bakersfield, Vermont
Mahogany
32" L x 14¾" H x 14" D
Private collection
Moran carved this chest as a birthday present for a friend's niece. The carving on it depicts the farm where she lives, including the house, barn and garage. The latter structure Moran had built, first measuring the car, then building the garage to fit around it.

Carved Rifle Stock
1961
Frank W. Moran,
Bakersfield, Vermont
Wood
13¼" L x 4½" H x 1½" D
Loaned by Mrs. James Beyor
Frank Moran carved several gun stocks. This was one of the last, finished on his eighty-fourth birthday.

Today most of Frank's carvings still remain in the Bakersfield area, quietly treasured and very definitely not for sale. But Frank became known beyond his home environs and visitors would come by the dozens every summer. At one time he had twenty cars in his yard at once. His best known work is his life-sized seated Lincoln which he carved from a solid piece of pine. "I roughed him out with a double bitted axe and then started carving. Took me almost a month to hollow out the chair and leave the rungs. I've got him sitting on a kitchen chair — figured he was a poor cuss, like me, and he'd feel right at home." While he was living he would never sell this statue, reputedly turning down $2,000 for it and stating "he won't ever stand up — or leave here."

This carving alone drew people. Many a person at first glance thought it was just another person sitting in his kitchen. In the end, the carving was sold to the New York State Historical Association at Cooperstown; a master's thesis was written on Frank Moran and he has taken his place among strangers, beyond his community, as a fine folk artist from Vermont.

Generally, however, folk art is seldom seen outside the local community. It is treasured and, therefore, seldom for sale. Sometimes it is given to the local historical society to insure its safety and preservation. Sometimes its functional use causes it to deteriorate — rugs and quilts receive heavy wear and tear, furniture takes the hard knocks of time. If an item is sold out of the family its context is quickly lost, but if it survives, it survives because of a different aesthetic value to a totally different audience. Thibault's bicycle sign now sits in a collector's apartment, appreciated for its workmanship and its novelty. "A wonderful piece" by New York standards, the sign commands a high price on the open market, its maker long forgotten except by name. Folk art in the public sphere is out of context. The object is admired for itself and is often described as "naive, unsophisticated, amateurish." Naive only to its new audience — an audience which no longer shares daily activities with the artist, but which instead looks upon many of these activities as "quaint."

Abraham Lincoln
c. 1940
Frank W. Moran,
Bakersfield, Vermont
Pine
4'7" H
Photograph courtesy of New York State Historical Association, Cooperstown
　　Moran's best known carving.

Greensboro Bend
1978
Roland Rochette,
Greensboro Bend, Vermont
Wood and cedar sprigs on paint
18" H x 25½" W
Loaned by the Town of Greensboro
　　This is a view of how Greensboro Bend looked in 1900. Roland Rochette did not live at the Bend then (he did not come until 1934) but Glenn Buck, a neighbor and someone Rochette introduced to painting, told him what it was like. As in all of Rochette's collages there is a lot going on. The railroad put Greensboro Bend on the map and was all important in carrying produce and cattle to urban markets. The railroad is also a favorite motif in Rochette's work, probably because of his association with the Canadian Pacific.

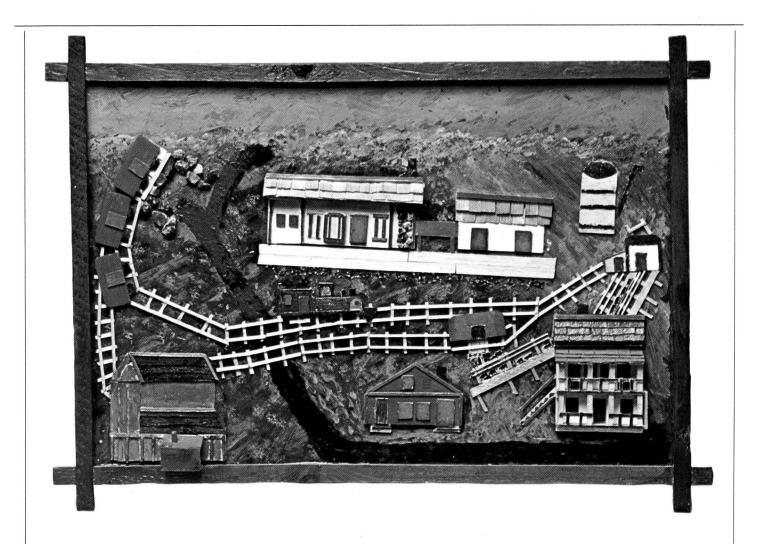

The collectors of folk art have substituted an economic value for the emotional bond that once existed in folk art. Tourists come to Vermont looking for handmade items to buy. This financial consideration has obviously had an impact on some of the folk art produced today. In general, it is still something done in quiet time, but because of its monetary worth, the item will be made for a different audience in order to supplement an income. When Roland Rochette retired at sixty-five he found he only received $64.00 a week from Social Security. As he told me,

"You don't go far with sixty-four bucks, you see. So, I heard about Grandma Moses. Well, I says, if a woman can do it, I can do it too. So I told my wife I'm going to try that. I didn't want to have any kind of help from the state. I wanted to be on my own, you see. Didn't want to go and say, well, I haven't enough to live. I thought, I'm going to help myself. Well, my first picture I had a big empty box. I cut the cardboard on it and I made a picture. It was horses out in a field. Had a granddaughter, she said 'Grandpa, would you give me that picture?' So I gave it to her. She says, 'I love it.' Over here they were raising money to pay for the church. So they had a bazaar and I told my wife, I says, 'Even if we don't sell it, I'm going to make a picture for the church and give it to them.' I made a picture of an old farm. I was out there in the country and I took (made) a picture of that farm. It didn't look like the people or the farm was making too good. Anyway there was a fellow from Connecticut and he bought it. And then, oh a week after that, he says 'I want you to come over to my summer place there and I want you not to try to straighten it up.' He bought an old place. He says, 'Just try to paint it. We'll pay you good.' 'Well,' I said, 'I don't care much about that — if you like it, buy it. If you don't, that will be all right.' I took the picture of his summer place and he loved it. So he bought it. And it started that way. And I wasted a lot of paint and then I thought, well — if I would do something else — I was not a painter, I never had any training. If I would glue some of them houses — collage, I call it — it would be something different, you see. So I made one. I made quite a few. So it started to go pretty good, you see, the people like that kind of stuff."

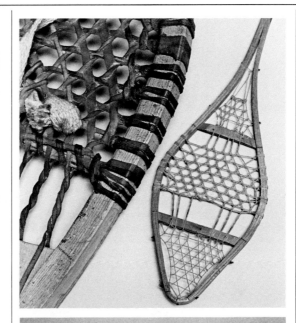

Snowshoes: Woman's and Miniature
c. 1925
Nikola Panadin, Quebec
St. Francis Abenaki
Ash, birch, rawhide, lampwick material, wool
35¾" L x 11" W (woman's)
8½" L x 2¾" W (miniature)
Loaned by the Hood Museum of Art, Dartmouth College

The miniature snowshoe, made for the resort trade, is shown here with an Abenaki woman's snowshoe. Despite its size, it was made true to Abenaki form. The miniature lacks the tufts of red wool yarn that adorn the adult's snowshoe. These wool tufts are a substitute for moose hair.

Many artists were surprised that people were interested in buying their work. A woman had seen a painting Marion Hastings had done and asked her if she could do another like it. Mrs. Hastings complied and when she gave it to her, the woman insisted on paying her $25.00. Mrs. Hastings confided, "I wouldn't have bought it for that." Since she was in the real estate business, many people were in and out of the old farm house and many of these clients were taken with her paintings and bought them.

Winfred Rhodes found that the whittling he did after he was laid off from his night watchman's job could work to his advantage.

"I went home, nothing to do, and I stayed around there off and on for about a week and then I said to my wife one day, 'I've got to have something to do or I'm going crazy.' So I went out and my son has a garage there and a work bench and I don't know how it happened, but I went to whittling and made a chair. Then I thought it would look nicer if it had arms on it, so I got to thinking what I could do and I made some extensions. There was a family right across the road, and the kids wanted to know if they could take the chair to school with them. So they took it in to school and brought it back the next night. Saturday, two ladies drove in and one of them was the school teacher that these kids went to and she said 'Could I buy a chair?' I said, 'I don't know as I got anything that would interest you.' I guess I had a couple made and was working on another… Well, I made some chairs and that's the way it started. They got them and then they told some friends and business was booming."

Of course, when an artist begins to make things to sell, his work is frequently responsive to what his customers buy. Collise Brown, a wood carver, said that generally he likes to carve traditional scenes like sugaring or a deer, because that's what he knows and sees every day, but it's also what the tourists are looking for. He went on to explain that the Rocky Mountain Billy Goat which he thought was his best carving, was something the tourists wouldn't look at twice because "it wasn't Vermont."

John Lawyer, conscious of his Abenaki and Mohawk heritage, shakes his head and says,

"I would travel down a different path if I didn't have to make what people will buy. People don't understand if I make something from my heritage. They understand pipes, western bead work. They like that. That's 'Indian' to them."

The understanding is gone. There is no longer any emotional link between the artist and the community he's creating for. Because John is "Indian" he produces something that is "Indian" for his non-Indian audience. What he would make for himself or his family would be very different.

Much of the Native American art in this exhibit has been influenced by outside forces. Miniature snowshoes and canoes are made in response to the tourist trade. While the miniatures are designed for the white man, the style and form is Abenaki. Indian work was particularly popular around the turn of the century and much of it is heavily influenced by Victorian styles that would appeal to resort customers. A beaded boot proved to be a very popular trade item. For some time it was thought to be typically Mohawk, but Abenakis traveling through Vermont also made and traded these same kinds of items. Basket styles were changed to appeal to customers, although the Indians maintained many of the old styles for themselves. Some of these baskets were made and traded for necessary items, like hay for their horses.

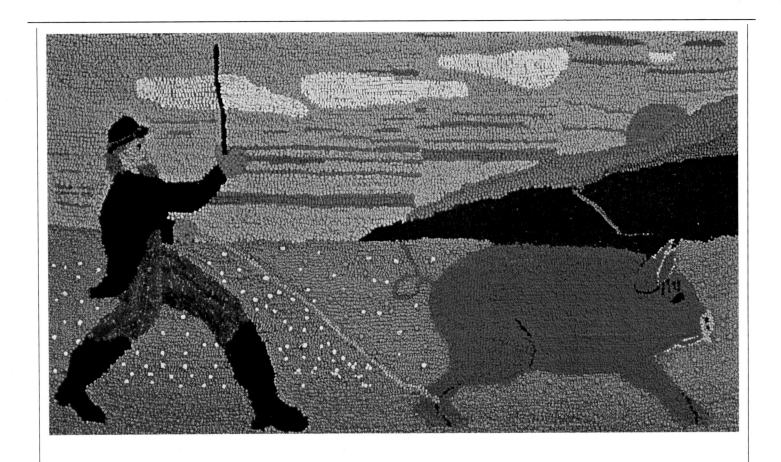

"Driving Hog to Market"
1978
Imelda Lepine,
Morrisville, Vermont
Woolen strips hooked
over burlap
23" H x 51" W
Loaned by Imelda Lepine

Imelda Lepine was born in Sherbrooke, Quebec and came to Elmore, Vermont to farm with her husband just after they were married in the early thirties. Life was hard and when they first moved to the farm they own today, they came with three cows and fifteen pigs. Fifteen pigs eventually became three hundred but these were lost almost overnight to a cholera epidemic. No strangers to adversity, the family simply worked all the harder. Mrs. Lepine has always hooked rugs since she learned from the nuns in Quebec. Using worn out woolen clothing, she has made both patterned and rugs of original design. When her son shot his first deer she presented him with a rug depicting his success. With more time now that her grown children run the farm for her, Mrs. Lepine has become well known in the neighborhood for her rug making and chair caning.

Beaded Pillow
c. 1885
Artist unknown, probably
Abenaki woman,
Brattleboro, Vermont
Fabric, beads
7¾" x 7¾"
Loaned by the Vermont
Historical Society

This is a good example of the Victorian influence that was reflected in many of the items the Abenakis and other Native Americans made for the resort trade around the turn of the century. Here native beadwork takes on a decidedly Victorian style.

Painted Fungus
c. 1900-1925
Artist unknown,
Woodford, Vermont
Fungus, oils
14" H x 27" W x 6" D
Loaned by the
Bennington Museum

This type of fungus was often gathered and used as material to either paint or carve. Few examples of this kind of art have been preserved. The scene is Woodford.

The Sweetsers, one of the best known basket-making families in Vermont, probably learned to make brown ash baskets from their Indian spouses. Today one of the family, Newton Washburn, still makes baskets. He first learned from his mother when he was eight in 1923 and continued to make them off and on until he went in the service in 1941. When he returned, he helped his uncle make a few, but then his uncle died and he turned to other things. He had been running a body shop for some twenty years when he had two heart attacks and was told he couldn't work any more. To while away the time he made his wife a laundry basket, then a couple of sewing baskets. As he says, "People saw them. There's no stop now, I guess."

In his early years, Washburn made baskets mostly for farmers. Today, his clientele has changed. With the revitalized interest in handcrafts, Washburn's baskets are in high demand. However, he has found that he must make certain concessions to his new clientele. They do not like the hooping nailed, something that the Sweetsers did traditionally. "I had half a dozen (baskets) here with the hooping nails in. Nobody wanted it. They said, 'Can't you bind it in?' Now I bind the hooping instead of nail it."

Neither did his buyers like the decorated baskets which the Sweetsers used to make. "I made some. I dyed a lot of filling my first year here. They didn't sell — you couldn't give them away. They want the natural wood." The same was true when he made some with curliques. Again he found that they were not what his buyers wanted. "But you got to sell them, so there's no need to making them." Once again, with the economic motive a major consideration, and the audience or clientele no longer the close knit local community, changes occur. The intimate relationship between artist and community is gone.

Horsebonnet
c. 1920
Artist unknown,
Newfane, Vermont
Straw
9" H x 13" Diam.
Loaned by the Historical Society
of Windham County

Some farm women used to
weave hats from buckwheat or
wheat for family members.
Before tractors, the horse was as
important as a family member.

Palm Leaf Hat
c. 1890-1900
Caroline Bartlett,
West Dover, Vermont
Palm leaves
4" H x 14½" Diam.
Loaned by Myrtle S. Ray

Mrs. Bartlett used to buy
palm leaf (something that
seems to have been available
only in southern Vermont) by
the pound. Making hats and
other fancy basketry was a
winter-time activity and a means
of earning some extra money.
Even the small children
would help with the easier parts
and by the time the girls were
ten they were making half a hat
a day. These hats would then
be sold to the local store or
to "somebody who came in
from outside."

"Our Town at Dawn"
1981
Cleland Selby,
Essex Junction, Vermont
Wool, burlap
3' H x 6' W
Loaned by Cleland E. Selby

Cleland is the third
generation of his family to
hook rugs and here he illustrates
his conception of a Vermont
village with school, church, mill,
sugar house, barns, cemetery,
covered bridge, stores and
houses.

Nevertheless, the economic motive must be reckoned with in folk art. It changes the context, but it also acts as a further stimulus. Today few people will resist the opportunity to supplement an income shrinking from inflation. The artist now has two audiences — his own family, friends and neighbors and the people from "down country" who come looking for his art. The first treasure his creations because they mean something both aesthetically and emotionally, the second because of a nostalgic, romantic attitude toward the maker, and the potential economic value.

The trend is not new. As early as 1860, Mrs. Newton, the wife of the local minister in Marlboro, is said to have introduced the making of palm leaf hats. Peddlers sold palm leaves for twelve and one-half cents a pound and local women bought them, wove hats and then sold them back to the peddler for eight cents a hat. It became a thriving cottage industry in southern Vermont which lasted until the first decade of the twentieth century when the palm leaves were no longer imported. The Reverend Newton refers to "braiding bees" in Marlboro where the women used to get together, socialize, and braid hats.

Another cottage industry was introduced into northern Vermont in the 1930's. A woman from Connecticut ("down country") arranged to have a number of Vermonters hook rugs for her in their spare time. She provided them with the materials and the patterns. They produced rugs and were able to supplement their income. One woman managed to put her four sons through college in this manner. At the same time she was making rugs for the Connecticut woman, she also saved scraps and made a few rugs of her own design for her family. During that time, one or two of her sons learned to hook. And today, her grandson, Cleland Selby, who can remember watching his mother and sometimes adding to her rug when she wasn't looking, designs and hooks rugs, with his wife, as "college money" for their three children.

Cleland's designs range over a wide spectrum. For a daughter, it might be Jemima, their family dog or perhaps a remembrance of their farm in Bridport, for strangers, variations on the Peaceable Kingdom. For the Selbys, rug hooking is not only a way to supplement an income, it is a shared family activity. The two older girls have completed a number of pieces, while the youngest, an eight-year-old boy, works sporadically on a parade of trucks. The stimulus is still the same. The artistic urge to create, the sense of tradition behind the work is there still. But there is also the economic incentive and a wider "foreign" audience which is no longer intimately concerned with the artist and his everyday activities.

What then is Vermont folk art today? It is still art done in a quiet moment by people living a traditional lifestyle, sharing activities with family and neighbors and depending on traditional learning rather than formal academic training in art. This art reflects that lifestyle and is usually made with what outsiders would think of as insignificant materials — materials that are inexpensive and easily available. Today, for example, a braided rag rug might be constructed out of plastic bread bags. It is an art shaped by a Vermont environment and indicative of Vermont activities. It is largely representative or narrative in impulse. It is active rather than passive; conservative rather than innovative; representational rather than cryptic; concrete rather than abstract. It is a vision that is shared by a tightly knit community and when this vision is accepted beyond the community, it is looked upon in different terms. There is no longer the same emotional bond. The aesthetics have become all important and the aesthetics of the outsider may well be different from those of the local community — hence the terms "naive, amateurish and quaint."

While the collector tends to view a piece of folk art as naive in its conception, but aesthetically pleasing in its construction, something perhaps with symbolic and impressionistic overtones, the man who used to roll the roads looks at the miniature snow roller and exclaims, "That's just about perfect. That's what I call art."

Jane C. Beck
Vermont Folklorist

The Native American Legacy

The Native American Legacy

Since the beginning of the Republic of Vermont in the eighteenth century, Vermonters have been taught that this land was an uninhabited wilderness before the coming of the Europeans. Census records since 1790 have supported this idea by consistently showing the lowest native American population of any state in the Union, never recording more than sixty Indians residing in Vermont from 1790 to 1960. But then in 1980, the Federal Census Bureau recorded almost one thousand Native Americans living in the state, a dramatic change which does not reflect a real shift in the population but rather a new understanding of the extensive tradition and history of the original inhabitants of the Green Mountains.

Research in archaeology, anthropology, genealogy and oral history over the past twenty-five years has established that Vermont has been occupied by native peoples for at least eleven thousand years. It is now reasonable to assume that as many as ten thousand Abenaki and Mahican peoples lived in upwards of twenty villages in Vermont when Columbus "discovered" the New World.[1] Far from being a no-man's land until the European settlements began, Vermont may well have served as a refuge for hundreds or thousands of Indians during the expansion of British rule in North America.

Vermont history is being rewritten further by the historical and genealogic research conducted by several scholars in the Abenaki Identity Project and Abenaki Research Project.[2] Extensive family biographies pursued through interviews are helping to shed light on a number of historical misconceptions. One of these is the story of Robert Rogers and his one hundred fifty rangers who, under the orders of Sir Jeffery Amherst, were to exterminate the Indian "scourges" of New England. Until recently it was believed that all of the St. Francis Abenaki who were living in their mission village at Odanak, Quebec were killed by Rogers' Rangers. Oral history complemented by documentary evidence reveals that there were indeed hundreds of survivors. Until now the history of the Native American in Vermont has been written by the white man but today, through these oral histories, a different voice is heard.

For many thousands of years before the white man, the Wabanaki or Abenaki (People of the Dawnland) lived in Vermont. In 1609, Samuel de Champlain discovered the lake which bears his name, but confused future historians by describing the large corn fields in the Champlain Valley as the lands of the Iroquois. The best evidence available now suggests that it was the Abenakis, not the Mohawks of the Iroquois Confederacy, who tended these fields.[3] Oral tradition originating in Swanton, Vermont and passed from Indian to white in the early 1800's shows clearly that there were thriving villages of Abenakis at Missisquoi (Swanton-Highgate), St. Albans, Milton, and the Intervales in Burlington in 1613.[4] Ancient oral tradition from both the Abenakis and the Mohawks tell of Odziozo, the Abenaki hero who transformed the Champlain Valley and surrounding mountains, then turned himself into Rock Dunder in Burlington Bay so he could survey his fine creation forever. And even the St. Francis Abenakis, who left Vermont by 1800 for the safety of their Canadian reserve at Odanak, still consider Vermont and New Hampshire to be the center and source of their ancient tradition.

[1]William A. Haviland and Marjory W. Power, **The Original Vermonters**, Hanover, N.H.; The University Press of New England, 1981, p. 155.
S. F. Cook, **The Indian Population of New England in the Seventeenth Century**, Berkeley, Cal. University Press, 1976, p. 84. Henry Dobyns, "Estimating Aboriginal American Population," **Current Anthropology**, vol. 7, no. 4, 1966, pp. 359.

[2]The Abenaki Identity Project was established by the Canadian Ethnology Service of the National Museums of Canada

The Abenaki Research Project was founded in 1977 by the Abenaki Nation/Vermont to research their ancestry and tribal history. Since then an extensive ethno-historical archive has been developed at the offices of the tribe in Swanton, Vermont.

Container with Lid
? Late 19th century
Susanna Wheeler,
Eastern Woodland,
Algonkian, Vermont
Birch bark, spruce root,
vegetable dye
9¼″ H x 6¾″ Circum.
Loaned by the Hood Museum
of Art, Dartmouth College

This container is made of traditional, indigenous materials and is in the traditional form of a bark canister, but the artisan's signature indicates it to have been made for sale to white clientele.

In the early years of white settlement, 1609 to 1759, the Abenakis followed a lifestyle dating back hundreds or even thousands of years. At Missisquoi (Place of the Flint), Winooski (Place of the Onion), Coos (Place of the Pines), and other sites, the Abenakis had large villages, which are described by European accounts after 1680.[5] The people of these villages followed an annual cycle not very different from the way their descendants, and other Vermonters, hunt, fish, farm, and gather food in rural areas today. They fashioned from the earth, animals, and plants all that subsistence and ceremonial demands required, including the baskets, traps, snowshoes, moccasins, and other objects shown in this exhibit. Hunting, fishing, trapping, gathering, sugaring, raising corn, squash, and other foods kept them closely linked to the natural world. Much of the staple garden and farm produce still grown in Vermont was passed on to early colonial settlers by the Abenakis and their northeastern kin during the long periods of peace.[6]

But, although the essentials of village life remained unchanged during the early years of European settlement, the need for European knowledge, for guns, iron, cloth and even liquor became a matter of survival for the Abenaki. Similarly, Europeans needed furs, food, medicine, tobacco, permission to use the land, and Indian knowledge of the lakes, rivers, forests and fields. Trading relationships with the Europeans in French Quebec and English New England became very important to the Abenakis of Vermont in the seventeenth century.

[3]Gordon M. Day. "The Eastern Boundary Iroquoia: Abenaki Evidence," **Man in the Northeast** 1:8, 1971.

[4]Julia C. Smalley, "Traces of an Indian Legend," **The Catholic World** 22:277-81, 1876.

[5] Day, p. 9

[6] John Moody, Field Notes 1977-81.
Archives, Abenaki Nation/Vermont, Swanton, Vermont.
John Moody, "Missisquoi: Abenaki Survival in their Ancient Homeland," unpub. MS, 1979.

Lake Champlain and the surrounding highlands were considered some of the best beaver trapping grounds in the region and the trade in pelts was the basis of exchange with traders such as William Pynchon and others in Massachusetts Bay and Quebec. An economy based on this trade became the pattern upon which several northeastern tribes relied for some of their income, and which is still part of many of these tribes' contemporary lifestyles.

Yet by 1700, the fur trade from Vermont was in a steady decline as the Great Lakes region and other more northerly and westerly sources became the focus of French and English attention. Vermont became more important as a corridor for trade and warfare between Quebec and the English colonies of New York and Massachusetts Bay. The major bands of Abenakis, the Mazip-skoiak (People of the Flint Place) and Winoskoiak (People at the Onion River) on Lake Champlain and the Coasiak (People at the Pines) on the Connecticut River, became intermediaries in that trade. The Abenakis continued to demand, and receive, the right to protect their ancient homeland and therefore kept it free from European settlements through much of the 1700's.

By far the most valuable commodity to the English settlements of Massachusetts was the Abenakis' ancient homeland. In southern Vermont, land purchase or rental from the Indians was followed until about 1730. At that point, the Abenakis drew a clear line in their treaties with the colonists from Fort Number 4, near present day Springfield, Vermont, to the coast of Maine at Saco. North of that line they would not give permission for hunting, fishing, lumbering or settlement by whites. The English colonists, of course, disagreed and the long series of battles for colonial Vermont which shaped this state were waged over the next fifty years. In northern Vermont, the French, and later the English and Dutch colonists had agreed several times to rent from and cooperate closely with the Abenakis when using their lands. Thus, while the Abenaki considered all of central and northern Vermont their home, the larger communities were forced to stay in northern Vermont and Canada during wartime to assure the tribe's survival.

Beaded Draw Purse
c. 1900
Artist unknown, Abenaki, Proctor, Vermont
Leather, beads
5″ H x 4″ W
Loaned by Mrs. Arthur Mead

Mrs. Mead remembers an "Indian" family coming through Proctor one summer and pitching a tent and camping down near Otter Creek. Her grandmother used to buy things from them. Among the items was this beaded draw purse.

Quilled Birch Bark Box
19th century
Artist unknown,
Eastern Woodland, Algonkian
Birch bark, quills, thread, dye
3¾″ H x 4⅜″ Circum.
Loaned by the Hood Museum of Art, Dartmouth College

Most of the birch bark quill work seems to have been of Micmac origin. Originally the Micmacs used quills and moose hair to ornament leather clothing. These boxes, an adaptation of the earlier form, became a popular item for the resort trade. Because of its relatively early date of manufacture and collection, this particular piece is "contact" rather than "tourist" art.

Covered Basket
c. 1865-1890
Artist unknown, Abenaki,
South Walden, Vermont
Brown ash
12″ H x 11″ W x 11″ D
Loaned by Elizabeth White

"Gypsies" used to winter in South Walden every year near the railroad tracks. The local farmers used to raise a good crop of hay and the "Gypsies" would come up and trade baskets in exchange for hay for their horses.

By 1700, on the frontier of Indian country around Brattleboro, Vermont and Northfield, Massachusetts, another economic pattern was emerging. Indians living close by white settlements began making baskets, brooms, tool handles and other items to peddle to the settlers. They also hired on as laborers to help those settlers clear and farm land. As European encroachments grew in Vermont, this pattern would become the major means by which the Abenakis would survive and maintain their tribal identity and heritage . Behind the obvious exchange of money for services or tools, Indians and colonists carried on an extensive exchange of knowledge and skills necessary to the survival of each.

Each new wave of colonists who entered Vermont from the southern and northern routes in the course of the eighteenth and early nineteenth century reported close association with the Abenakis in frontier areas. As the land was taken from the tribes by force, Abenaki families became more and more reliant on the protection of European "friends" usually French and Dutch and increasingly dependent upon established trade relationships. Few of the newcomers knew the ways of the land so the Abenakis gave them guidance in all the intricacies. Maple sugaring, crop raising, berry and wild food gathering, trapping, hunting, fishing, plus the extensive trading relationship for furs, herbs, baskets, tools, cloth, weapons, and even food continued.[7] Guiding became a central role of the Indian with successive generations of newcomers. And not surprisingly, medicine based on the extensive healing knowledge of the Abenakis, using skills long rejected or unknown in Europe, became a basic medium of exchange. French, Indian, and metis (mixed blood) communities grew in many former Abenaki villages like Salisbury, Vergennes, Charlotte, Burlington, Colchester, Milton, the Islands, St. Albans, Georgia and Swanton, as well as Newbury, Hinesburg, Braintree, Randolph and many other towns.[8] It appears that Indians lived in almost every river town on both sides of the Green Mountains from the late 1700's on with the central and northern portions of the state having larger concentrations.

[7]Ibid.
[8]Ibid.

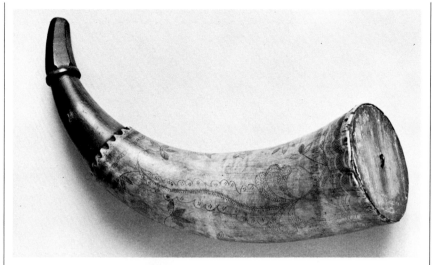

Powder Horn
c. 1778
Artist unknown, Indian?
Abenaki? Vermont
Horn
8″ L x 3½″ W
Loaned by the Marlboro Historical Society

There is no firm documentation on this powder horn, only the story that it was given as a gift to an ancestor of Bertha Rider Moore during the Revolutionary War. It is known that horns were decorated by Native Americans and were also used as dance rattles. A floral design of realistic flower figures might well be used by a Native American.

Powder Horn
c. 1777
Captain Titus Watson,
St. Albans, Vermont
Horn and wood
4″ H x 14″ L x 7″ W
Loaned by the Franklin County Museum and Philip B. Meigs

Titus Watson was a member of a pioneer family of St. Albans. His powder horn depicts both Fort Ticonderoga and Mt. Independence on either side of Lake Champlain with the connecting bridge and boom.

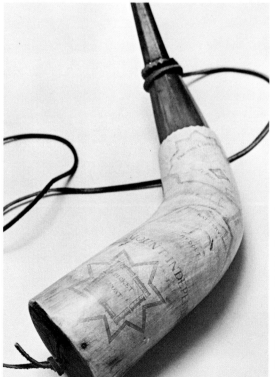

Card Case
19th Century
Artist unknown,
Eastern Woodland, Algonkian
Birch bark, quill, thread, dyes
3½" H x ¾" W x 2¾" D
Loaned by the Hood Museum
of Art, Dartmouth College

Here is another example of
an adaptation of Micmac quill
work. Again, because of its
relatively early date of manufacture and collection, it is
"contact" rather than tourist art.

Birch Bark Quilled Box
c. 1906-7
Christena Mary Foster,
Mount Mansfield, Vermont
Birch bark, 1500 porcupine
quills and raffia
5" H x 4½" W x 5" D
Courtesy of
Mrs. Bessie Foster Harlow

According to her daughter,
Mrs. Foster first saw quilled birch
bark boxes which the Indians
(most probably Micmacs)
brought to sell for souvenirs on
top of Mount Mansfield. Her
brother owned a mountain
house and she was the cook.
She was artistically inclined and
decided to try it herself. She
went and gathered her birch
bark, killed some hedgehogs
and went to work. She poured
boiling water over the quills,
letting them "set" until the water
cooled and then pulled them
out. It is interesting to note that
Mrs. Foster's mother was Indian
and that from her she learned
a great deal about gathering
herbs for medicine.

It was in the north, as well, that intermarriage,
the third major change in Indian-European
relationships began sometime in the late eighteenth century. English colonists were sometimes
adopted after being captured by Indians, but
there was very little intermarriage until the
beginning of the nineteenth century. The French
and Dutch however, began intermarrying with
Vermont Indians as early as the 1600's. Most of
Vermont's Indians spoke French as their second
language, and were nominally Catholic if they
practiced any European faith. This final step and
apparent acculturation was accompanied by
the Abenaki adopting the common dress and
semblance of European behavior to assure their
survival in a rapidly changing homeland. Until
recently, however, the dominant Anglo-American
scholarly community assumed that the "scourges"
of New England had withdrawn from the haunts
of civilization and vanished.

From Milton to Bedford, Quebec, Newbury,
Newburyport, and Memphremagog, the story of
the retreat and withdrawal of the original inhabitants of Vermont takes a similar form. After 1790-
1800, the "St. Francis Indians" that the Europeans
feared so long gradually "disappeared" into
Canada, the "wilds," or the "north." At the same
time, a relatively large population of poor, inter-
married, and very independent families appeared
in the records. The families were often French-
speaking and lived a basically nomadic life. They
were later called "gypsies" by both Indian and
whites in the early twentieth century. One family
recently traced was based in the Swanton area
but traveled from central Maine all the way to
New York State around Albany and the Akwesasne
Mohawk Reservation at Hogansburg, New York.

Other families stayed in one town or in a
much smaller radius for as long as they can remember or research can show. They were always
highly self-reliant families, who lived off the
available land as they had for centuries. Hunting,
fishing, trapping, gathering and trading continued
to sustain them. However, as they "disappear"
as Indians (after about 1830) they begin to emerge
in local records as laborers, traders, hunters,
woodworkers, tanners, cobblers, then later as
land-owning farmers, truckers, carpenters, and
masons.

Miniature Canoe
c. 1950
Artist unknown, Abenaki,
Thompson's Point, Vermont
Birch bark
11¾" L x 2½" W
Loaned by Mr. and Mrs. William
V. N. Carroll

One fall in the early 1950's, the Carrolls who summered at Thompson's Point, went to say good-bye to Marion and William Obomsawin. Their house was full of a great number of people weaving baskets. One man was making canoes and he gave the Carrolls one. Miniatures were popular tourist items and were also a stock in trade of William Obomsawin.

Sweet Grass Basket
c. 1935
Marion Obomsawin,
Thompson's Point, Vermont
Sweet grass
1¾" H x 5" L x 3½" W
Loaned by the Charlotte
Memorial Museum

These were used chiefly as sewing baskets and were made in various sizes. Most tribes of the Algonquin made them, but "none used the wide sweet grass braid as did the Abenaki." (Pelletier, p. 11)

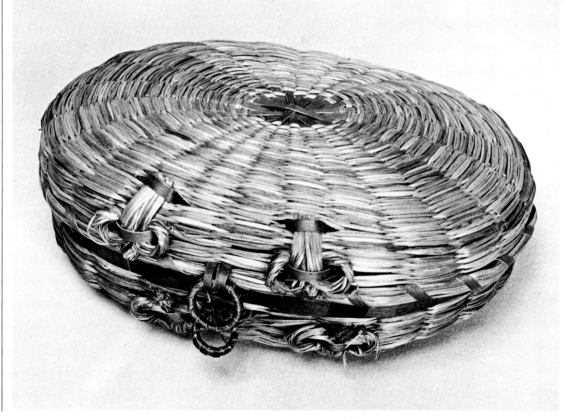

The Obomsawins

Simon Obomsawin, a member of a well-known Abenaki family, and his wife first came down
to Vermont in 1885. He put his canoe on a lumber barge and worked at unloading lumber on
Lake Champlain. They settled for the summer months at Cedar Beach where there was already
a tent colony and found they could capitalize on the summer resort trade. In the fall and winter months
they would return to Odanak and the north woods for hunting and to make baskets. (Simon's
wife also made splint ash hats.) In the summer months they came back to Vermont, selling
their wares on either side of Lake Champlain. Simon also gave demonstrations on weaving in full
Abenaki dress at roadside stores.

   It was after his wife died in 1890 that Simon was offered a more permanent job as caretaker
of the summer camps at Thompson's Point. He accepted, built himself a cottage and lived there with
two of his children, Marion and William. In the summer months he would take a boat across
the bay to pick up spring water and five gallons of milk for the summer residents and also peddle his
wares. Marion continued her father's tradition of making baskets and after a number of intervening
years which William spent in the north woods, he too returned and made items of trade with
his sister. They lived at Thompson's Point well into the 1950s making a variety of items which ranged
from baskets, book markers, miniature canoes, place mats to vases. (Courtesy of Gordon Day.) ●

By adapting to some of the white man's ways and becoming part of his economy, the Indian families were able to claim a portion of their homeland, neither incurring the wrath of the dominant society nor "disappearing" as the history books have long claimed. The Abenakis, and other Indians of the northeast who came to Vermont over the years lived at the periphery of the white man's consciousness. What was seen and understood by outsiders was what they needed to see, or what the Abenaki wished to reveal, and no more.

In many Vermont towns from 1780 to 1850 tales of local Indians abounded. There were the "good Indians" such as Indian Joe in Newbury and Captain John of Sherburne who held pensions from the state and federal government for fighting with the Vermonters during the Revolution. There were the "bad Indians," "them no-good St. Francis Indians" like Captain Louis who made a strong claim on behalf of his people to the village of Missisquoi at Swanton in 1788. There are the "last remnant" stories of families who "lingered here for many years" on some farm, in a swamp, in a remoter area only dimly recalled and sure to disappear by the 1840's. Mettalak and the last of the Cowasiaks from northwestern Vermont, Madam Camp and the last of the Mazipskoiaks from St. Albans, old Soison from Bellows Falls stand out. And there are the "old healer" traditions of Madam Crappo in St. Albans, Molly Orcutt in northwestern Vermont, and Sally Soisin in Bellows Falls which acknowledge the critical importance of Abenaki healing knowledge to early settlers. And, from every corner of the state, there are the occasional glimpses of the basket makers, the peddlers, who lived "close by" or in "Canada" and traded their wares for certain essentials only to disappear at will to some unknown retreat.

Just being heard now are descriptions of family and community traditions, and of people who remained behind, or journeyed faithfully each year to revered spots of economic support and deep personal significance. The Obomsawins of Charlotte, Grand Isle and Milton; the Panadis-Benedicts of Swanton and Highgate Springs; the Soisins of Bellows Falls; the Swassons, the Montagnes, Noels, Gardners, Phillips and Maurices of Lake Memphremagog and the Lawyers, St. Francis, Morits, Medors, Martins, Lazares, Freemores, and other families of northwestern Vermont are but a few.

The history of the Abenaki from the time of white settlement on, and their ability to adapt to the loss of control over their lands and to survive out of harm's way is made tangible by the baskets and other containers displayed in this exhibit. Abenaki artisans made a range of ash splint utility baskets which they could depend on selling to white people from the early 1800's down to the 1950's.

They also continued to make traditional birch containers, woven baskets made from a variety of plants, trees, and even hair, as well as pottery, fancy sweetgrass baskets, and more contemporary carved wooden containers. But it was the splint ash basketry which remained at the heart of Abenaki tradition, however much it may have been adapted to the nineteenth and twentieth century tourist-resort trade.

When tourist travel to the Lake Champlain-Richelieu corridor mineral springs and resorts became popular in the middle 1800's, some Abenaki families began to rely on the production and sale of baskets as their major source of cash. This trade continued into the middle 1900's, when a reduction in tourism and the importation of cheaper Asian-made baskets forced these artisans into other forms of work. However, with the great interest in handcrafts in the past ten to fifteen years, ash splint and fancy sweetgrass basketry has once again become a significant source of income for some families.

Container with Lid
? 18th century
Artist unknown,
Eastern Woodland, Algonkian,
possibly Abenaki, Vermont
Birch bark, spruce,
vegetable dye
7¾" H x 6-7¼" W x 11¼" D
Loaned by the Hood Museum
of Art, Dartmouth College

The container or "Mocock" is made from a single piece of birch bark which is folded and sewn with spruce root. These bark containers were used by the Eastern Algonkian to store fruits, vegetables, meat, grease, and small articles of clothing. Frequently ornamented with incised and painted designs, these bark containers were a typical and important part of Eastern Algonkian material culture. Incising was best done on bark peeled off during the winter. It would be wetted and heated until soft, then scraped down to the light layer upon which the design was incised with a bone or metal tool. A red-brown dye from alder bark was frequently applied to the entire surface. Grease also improved the appearance of the object. Pitch covering the seams made these containers water tight. ("The Arts of Native America, the Eastern Woodland: Algonkian and Iroquois, "Dartmouth College Museum and Galleries, March 6-November 11, 1979)

The need for practical utility baskets and the tradition of splint, twig, bark and woven basketry have been constant in Vermont, and are the basic tradition from which the tourist trade sprang. What the utility baskets lacked in fine handwork, they made up for in strength, function and durability. One and two-bushel, clothes, market, fish, egg, berry, bread, scrap and sewing baskets were made and sold in large numbers to a wide farm, home, and business clientele. Birch bark baskets were made during berrying season, right on the spot in the woods, and then the berries and basket both sold locally or shared in the community. Each Indian family made their own baskets which they peddled according to economic need in the immediate region around their homes. Furthermore, local tradition states that there was a clear agreement among Indian families to let one family per area make their basic living from the local trade. Another aspect of this same trade was caning chair bottoms or making snowshoes and a wide variety of related items.

There is some evidence that pottery, basketry, and beadwork for personal, community and ceremonial use has continued to be made in Vermont until the present. Accounts of handmade pottery, miniature coiled baskets made from horse or human hair, the hand drilling of shell pieces for traditional beads, the making of sheepshead bone necklaces and an assortment of other sacred objects used in northeastern Indian medicine and ceremonial tradition have appeared recently. To a large degree, it was the overlap between the tourist, utility and ceremonial basket making traditions which formed the backbone of the Abenaki economy in Vermont since 1800. With the food gathering techniques, strong affinity for the land, and medicine-midwifery practices, the Abenaki culture has remained a living tradition passed down through family and communities to the present. Today this legacy of Vermont's native people is being revealed as the Abenaki people begin to reaffirm their tribal identity in northwestern Vermont, an identity that was often overlooked but nevertheless durable.

John Moody
Abenaki Research Project

Basket with Lid
Early 20th century
Artist unknown, Abenaki,
Eastern Woodland
Willow, sweet grass, dyes
5¼" H x 7⅜" W
Loaned by the Hood Museum
of Art, Dartmouth College
   A "trinket" basket, this is
another example of the Abenaki
"marmot" basket.

Basket Creel
c. 1920
Artist unknown, Abenaki,
northern Vermont
Split hickory/ash, twisted
reed, sweet grass
9½" H x 14" L x 7" D
Loaned by Rayna Green
   According to Gaby Pelletier,
who has made a study of
Abenaki basketry, "The fishing
basket" as these creels were
known, does not appear in any
of the catalogs put out by
dealers who sold Abenaki
basketry. Apparently the
Abenakis, who claimed that
their husbands or fathers made
them "stated that they were
either made for personal use or
by special order." These
fishing baskets were commonly
made by the Maliseet, Passa-
maquoddy, Penobscot, and
Micmac tribes. (Pelletier, p. 44)

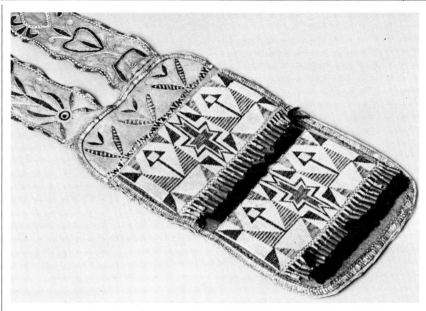

Pa-Tus-Se-Non (Shot Bag)
1810
Lizzette Harmon, Cree,
Bennington, Vermont
Porcupine quills, red floss,
leather
11″ H x 7″ W
Loaned by the
Bennington Museum

Daniel Harmon was born in Bennington in 1778. He spent most of his life in Canada working for the Northwest Company as an authorized agent, supervising the trading of merchandise for furs and for food supplies for the voyageurs and guides. In 1805, as was customary in those parts, he "took a squaw," Elizabeth (Lizzette) Laval, daughter of a French voyageur and a Cree Indian. When Harmon returned to Vermont, he legitimized their union through marriage, something that was not customary in the backwoods as it was the man's prerogative to leave his partner at any time and send her back to her family. This shot bag, decorated with naturally dyed porcupine quills, was made by Lizzette for her husband. (Levine, "Daniel Harmon," Part I and II)

Crooked Knife
c. 1900
Artist unknown, Abenaki?
Newport area, Vermont
Wood, rawhide, steel
9½″ L x 2¼″ W
Loaned by Mrs. Claire Blanchard

This crooked knife was given to Mrs. Blanchard's father by an Indian. The design has been carefully incised and then a wax-like substance seems to have been inserted while in liquid form. The colors of red, green and blue have maintained their brilliance. This would not be a resort trade item.

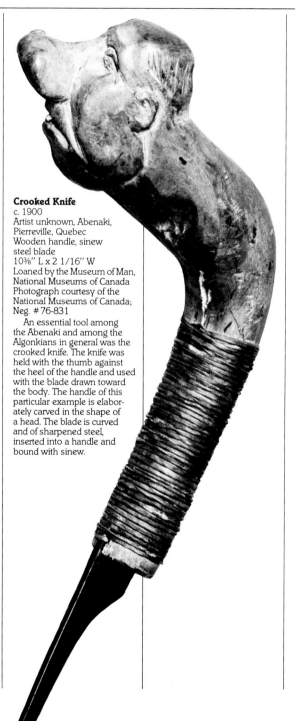

Crooked Knife
c. 1900
Artist unknown, Abenaki,
Pierreville, Quebec
Wooden handle, sinew
steel blade
10⅜″ L x 2 1/16″ W
Loaned by the Museum of Man,
National Museums of Canada
Photograph courtesy of the
National Museums of Canada;
Neg. #76-831

An essential tool among the Abenaki and among the Algonkians in general was the crooked knife. The knife was held with the thumb against the heel of the handle and used with the blade drawn toward the body. The handle of this particular example is elaborately carved in the shape of a head. The blade is curved and of sharpened steel, inserted into a handle and bound with sinew.

Crane
c. 1930
Artist unknown,
Champlain Valley, Vermont
Wood
37" H x 3½" W x 15" D
Loaned by Joe Duggan

A confidence decoy used around Lake Champlain. This is a rare example seldom found in Vermont.

Hen Whistler Decoy
c. 1900
George H. Bacon,
Burlington, Vermont
Wood, painted
5¾" H x 12½" L x 5" W
Loaned by Joe Duggan

Bacon was a well known decoy maker in the Champlain Valley and is thought to have made several hundred during his lifetime (1861-1925). His decoys are characterized by the placement of the eyes high on the head. (Webster and Kehoe, p. 44)

Loon
1981
Earl Cheney, Newport, Vermont
Wood, painted
9½" H x 17" L x 5" W
Courtesy of Mr. and Mrs. Ted Chaffee

Earl Cheney carved his first duck decoy when he was twelve. His uncle, after telling him he was good enough with a knife to make his own, refused to lend Earl any decoys. The boy went to work and made forty. Although Earl has worked with wood sporadically throughout his life, it wasn't until after he retired that it became a full-time occupation. Now he spends most of his waking hours in his shop carving an assortment of items. Ducks have been his most popular but "as I can get awful sick of making ducks" he has tried his hand very successfully at a variety of things: draft horses, owls, religious figures and most recently, loons.

Drake and Hen
Bluebill Decoys
c. 1930
Archie Bodette,
Vergennes, Vermont
Wood, painted
Hen: 6" H x 13" L x 6" W
Drake: 5½" H x 14" L x 5¾" W
Loaned by Joe Duggan

Archie Bodette was both a hunter and trapper and made quite a number of decoys, mostly for his own use.

Redhead Hen Decoy
c. 1831
Frank Owens,
South Burlington, Vermont
Wood, painted
7¼" H x 13½" L x 6⅛" W
Loaned by the Shelburne Museum

This is an early example of a solid decoy from the Lake Champlain area. Frank Owens was a stonemason in South Burlington.

Goose Decoy
c. 1880's
Isaac Wells, Milton, Vermont
Wood, painted, tin base
18¼" H x 9½" W x 24" L
Loaned by Duane Merrill

Isaac Wells (1840-1910) lived right on the shores of Lake Champlain where he was a commercial fisherman. He was also an avid hunter.

Water Fowl Decoys

The Indians are generally believed to have introduced Europeans to the use of decoys. It is interesting to note that the first written record of their use in North America was made by a French explorer when he visited Lake Champlain in 1685. These first decoys were of skins and feathers. The settlers adopted the device, but chose to carve them out of wood, thereby making decoys which could be used over and over.

Moccasins
1981
John Lawyer,
St. Albans, Vermont
Leather, beads, and cotton
11" L x 4" W
Loaned by John Lawyer

John Lawyer

John Lawyer's ancestry is rooted in northwestern Vermont and nearby southern Quebec. His father Peter had ties to both the Abenaki and the Mohawk Indians. Throughout his life Peter made different types of splint baskets as well as very small coiled horsehair baskets which his mother had made before him and which John says were popular for use on watch fobs. Coiled basketry actually predates splint basketry in the northeast and coiled mats and baskets are still made for ceremonial use in Akwesasne. John's father was also an accomplished wood and leather worker and generally made his living as a carpenter, cobbler or peddler in northwestern Vermont.

John himself has turned to shoe repair as his bread and butter, but he is a fine artisan working in a variety of mediums — doing anything from wood and soapstone carving to feather and bead work. Some of these items are for sale at his shop in St. Albans. These pieces are mostly what the outsider would recognize as "Indian," much as the resort trade items at the turn of the century appealed to the tourists. There are also things which John likes to make only for his own use, or perhaps his wife's. Moccasins are a good example. He made his first pair when he was ten — cutting out the leather and sewing them right on his foot.

Since then he has made several pairs. The toe patch he beaded over very thin cloth about twelve years ago and has worn them on three different sets of moccasins. The design of the growing plant on the toe piece has always been an important motif among the Abenaki, signifying the power of the plant world with all its spiritual, medicinal, and life-giving properties. In his own life, John follows his traditions and heritage. To the outside world, he gives what they think of as Indian. As he says, "I would travel down a different path if I didn't have to make what people will buy. People don't understand if I make something from my heritage. They understand pipes, western bead work. They like that. That's Indian to them." Thus like many of his ancestors, he preserves two traditions — his own and what others believe is his. ●

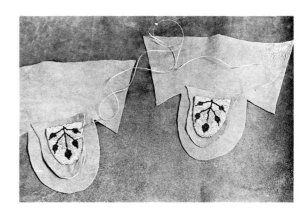

Brown Ash Basket
1981
Newton Washburn,
Littleton, New Hampshire
Brown ash
8¾" H x 14½" Diam.
Loaned by Jane Beck

A half bushel basket made with natural colors. The chain link design is made with the brown ash nearest the bark. This is the whitest in color and is known as the sap ring. Note the bound hooping.

Brown Ash Market Basket
c. 1930
Frank G. Sweetser,
Stowe, Vermont
Brown ash
5¾" H x 8¼" W x 15¾" L
Loaned by Perley D. Sweetser

This is a market basket which along with the one and two bushel-size baskets were among the most popular that the Sweetsers made. Three red-colored strips are made with dye from berries. Note the hooping which is nailed, not bound, as Newton Washburn does now because of popular taste.

Pack Baskets
Photograph courtesy of the Vermont Historical Society

Members of the Sweetser family making brown ash pack baskets — another popular item. c. 1920
Front Row: William Sweetser, his dog, and John Sweetser
Back Row: Arthur Tiff and his sister-in-law Gertrude Sweetser (John Sweetser's wife)

From Generation to Generation

The Sweetser family has been well known for its baskets since at least 1850 and probably before. The original Sweetser is said to have come from Switzerland to Vermont. His son married an Indian woman, Lydia Hill, and their son, Gilman Sweetser, born in 1820 became the man in living memory who taught his children how to make baskets.

Three generations later, Newton Washburn, great grandson of Gilman Sweetser is still making baskets in the same tradition, which includes fancy baskets, women's work baskets, half-bushel and bushel baskets, clothes baskets, market baskets, fish baskets, pack baskets, even cradles. Newton first started in 1923 when he was eight, shaving the brown ash strips with a knife (it was usually the men's job to pound the brown ash log, removing the strips from the log). He next graduated to setting up the bottoms. By the time he was nine, he was making the whole basket, not only laying the uprights for the bottom, but tipping up the ends to form the sides, weaving the filler strips into place, and nailing the hoops and handles to the rim.

Newton learned his techniques from his mother who made mostly fancy baskets and trained young Newton, telling him "You make it right or you make it over." She taught him two different types of bottoms — the Demijohn bottom coming down from the Sweetsers and the star bottom from his Abenaki grandmother. She also taught him how to turn all the uprights — another Abenaki tradition according to Newton, rather than cutting off every other one to make the basket stronger and so that it could still be used without the hooping. She showed him the different ways to make dyes — purple from hemlock bark, yellow from goldenrod and red from berries or beets and such designs as the chain link or diamond.

Baskets were made mostly in the winter and not infrequently served as a family activity in the long evenings. However, if an unexpected visitor should appear, everything would be swept aside as this was very much a Sweetser activity and never taught outside the family. These baskets were traded for groceries during the winter and after the spring's work was done, the men of the family would take off, selling or trading them for pigs, chickens or any other useful item. By 1933 or 1934 Newton's family all but stopped making baskekts, for galvanized containers had been introduced and the farmers felt these were better. Only his Uncle Frank continued and Newt helped him off and on until 1945 when his uncle's health failed.

Newton set aside his basket making and for over twenty years ran a body shop until he was slowed by two heart attacks. Recovering, and wanting something to do, he decided to make his wife a laundry basket, then two sewing baskets and before he knew it, he was off on a new career. People saw his baskets and wanted them. Furthermore, they wanted to learn his art. Knowing the old Sweetser feeling about this, Newton went to a member of the older generation questioning "What am I going to do? Let it drop or teach it? If somebody doesn't the art's going to go." "Well," came the answer, "we never did. But use your own judgment." Since that time Newt has had over sixty apprentices.

Brown Ash Cradle
1981
Newton Washburn,
Littleton, New Hampshire
Brown ash
39″ H x 20″ L x 11½″ W
Loaned by Newton Washburn

Newton Washburn, who grew up in Stowe, remembers his mother, Loula Sweetser making cradles — "They always sold" — and today produces a replica, as he had been taught. He explained that sometimes the canopy was made so that it could swing from one side to the other and pointed out that the double hooping in front of the canopy was for extra strength.

Basket
Early 20th century
Artist unknown, Abenaki,
Eastern Woodland
Willow, sweet grass or
holy grass, dye
12⅜″ H x 10¼″ W
Loaned by the Hood Museum
of Art, Dartmouth College

An excellent example of a
non-traditional shape of basket
made for the resort trade.

73.

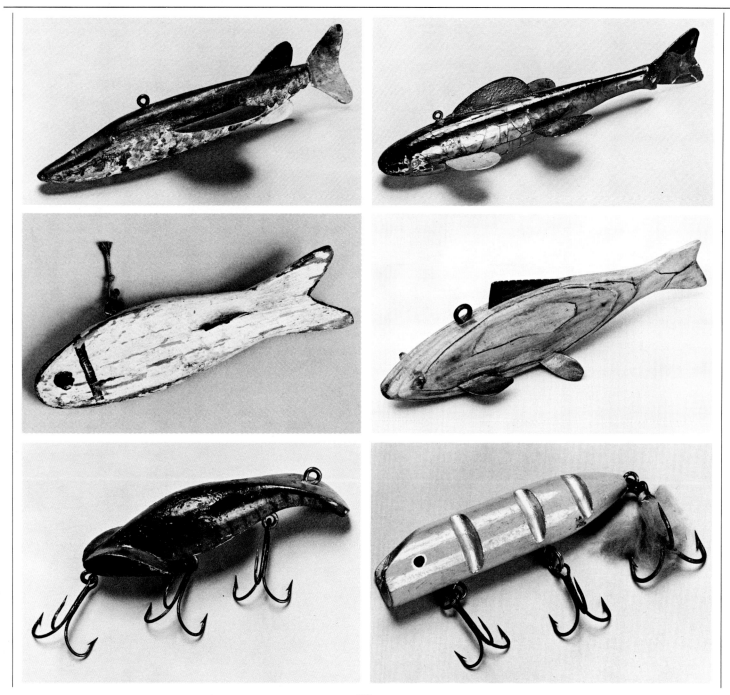

Fish Decoy
c. 1915-1925
Artist unknown, Vermont
Wood, painted, tin
7″ L x 3″ W
Loaned by Seth Rosenbaum
   A fish decoy used for pike.

Fish Decoy
c. 1915-1925
Artist unknown, Vermont
Wood, painted, tin
7½″ L x 2¼″ W
Loaned by Seth Rosenbaum
   A fish decoy used for trout.

Fish Decoy
c. 1900
Rita Corey, Brandon, Vermont
Wood, tin, painted
6″ L x 1½″ W
Loaned by Tim Stevenson

Fish Decoy
c. 1930
Artist unknown, Vermont
Wood
5½″ L x 1½″ W
Loaned by Gregg Blasdel

Fish Lure
c. 1920-1930
Artist unknown, Vermont
Wood, painted
4½″ L x 1″ Diam.
Loaned by Seth Rosenbaum
   This lure is carved to resemble a baby pike and was used for bass, walleye and northern pike.

Fish Lure
c. 1920-1930
Artist unknown, Vermont
Wood, painted
4⅜″ L x 1″ Diam.
Loaned by Seth Rosenbaum
   This is known as a "teaser lure" (possibly a yellow perch) and was probably used on Lake Champlain for bass, walleye and northern pike.

Fish Decoys

In Vermont fish decoys have been found mostly around Lake Champlain, although they could have been used in any lake or pond where there is ice fishing. It is said that these decoys were first introduced by the Indians and were most popular up to the 1920's. Today they are rapidly disappearing. Few people still fish with them, and fewer make them. They were used to attract the fish — perch, walleye, smelt, pike, and trout. Handcarved, usually with fins made from tin cans, some were painted many colors, others simply white or gray with red eyes. Still others were made as careful replicas of the fish the ice fisherman wished to catch. ●

Jig Sticks
c. 1968
Bob Bearor,
Chittenden, Vermont
Wood
17″ H x 3″ W x ⅜″ D
Loaned by Bob Bearor
   Bob Bearor has long been an avid ice fisherman. In his spare time, he spends hours carving, sanding, laminating and then seizing his jig sticks with twine. He gets whistles of approval when other fishermen see him using one of his own sticks and he has had many offers to buy. But for Bob Bearor these items are not for sale.

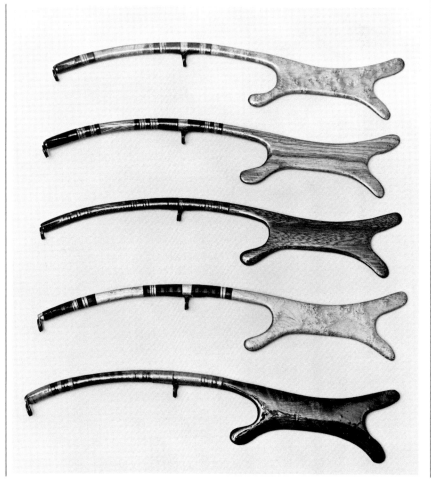

Farmstead and Family Life: "One for the Blackbird ...One for the Crow"

"One for the Blackbird…"

One hesitates to add yet another leaf to the extant mountain of scribblings about Vermont and Vermonters. There is, however, a mythic view of the state abroad in the world and it needs remedying. Seemingly it has been difficult to write unemotionally about the Old Green Mountain State which has slowly vanished over the years under the weight of stereotypes foisted upon it by promotional types and others who might have known better.

It's a pretty heavy burden being mythologized. On the whole Vermonters have borne up well and met it halfway. They've seen the humor in it and gone along when it wasn't too much of a nuisance. I suppose they felt that if people from away were damn fools enough to believe everything they read about Vermont, it wasn't their responsibility to disillusion them. So it's finally come to where the countryside of the state is almost universally assumed to be just like a **Vermont Life** calendar.

As for the Natives, it is widely accepted that to a man they were spare, tenacious, taciturn, frugal, wryly humorous and stonily independent (and often as not, stony broke). The women, too, of course, and the children were expected to grow up that way.

If we are to gain any genuine understanding of the objects of folk art composing this exhibit beyond their three-dimensional aspects, we should know something of the complexities of the real Vermont and its folk past. The fact is that Vermont and Vermonters have warts just like any other place and people. For the major portion of her brief history the state has suffered from a malady called Economic Depression. In the little villages and out on the back roads one can find poverty as bitter as anywhere in the United States. And while the lifestyle has indeed produced a disproportionate share of men and women to whom the stereotype applies, it has also broken a good many others and caused enormous numbers of young people to emigrate over the years.

Comparing the present with even the not too distant past can be instructive. Over the last twenty years the idea of "Country Living" has become a hot item of urban culture and lots of folks have moved up here. Fifteen or twenty years ago, when a wealthy incomer mentioned he had just laid a new stone wall or split a cord of wood, the native was inclined to believe he'd done it with his own hands, for he had long been well accustomed to do such things for himself. It took a while for it to sink in that what the city man meant was that he'd hired someone else to do it for him.

"Highland Home Farm"
Mid 1950's
Norris Barton,
New Haven, Vermont
House paint on plywood
1' H x 4' W
Loaned by Winston and
Isabelle Swain

Norris Barton, probably born about 1905 — some say in Barton, others in Rutland — traveled the state painting on barns, on general stores, or anywhere someone was willing to have him paint. For a time he lived in New Haven near "Highland Home Farm" and the Swains commissioned him to paint their farm for $5.00. They provided a piece of plywood and "for the better part of the forenoon" Barton sat across the road painting the farm buildings, including some ducks. Barton has been known as "Dog Man" because in his later years he used to drive a team of dogs pulling a cart, or in some cases as "Bicycle Pete." It is said that he used to ride his bicycle to Florida in the winter. (Fried and Fried, pp. 116-120)

Merino Ram Weathervane
c. 1860
Artist unknown,
Cornwall, Vermont
Copper
3½" H x 3' W
Loaned by Arlyn Foote

In the mid-nineteenth century, the Champlain Valley became a cradle for Merino sheep. Among the breeders was Rockwell Foote of Cornwall, who traveled several times to Australia to sell some of his sheep. When he built a sheep barn in 1860 he had a Merino ram weathervane put atop it as a symbol of his major interest. Four generations later the switch has been made from Merinos to Holsteins but the ram still symbolizes the original focus of the farm.

Hooked Rug
c. 1930
Alma Davis, Johnson, Vermont
Wool over burlap
32" x 20"
Loaned by Mrs. Sybil Sweet

Mrs. Davis made a large number of hooked rugs, usually drawing her own designs and always using woolen rags of well-worn clothing for her material. This particular rug shows the house that she was born in.

Cow Weathervane
1980
Duncan Hastings,
Swanton, Vermont
Steel, painted black
45" H x 30" W
Loaned by the Billings
Farm Museum

Duncan Hastings learned his trade traditionally by apprenticing himself to Percy Bliss of Perkinsville. He patterned this weathervane after an old butter print of a cow and hand forged it.

Crazy Quilt
c. 1865
Mrs. Samuel Glover Haskins,
Rochester, Vermont
Cotton, appliqued
88" L x 79½" W
Loaned by
Mrs. Louise Haskins Stiles

This quilt is a patchwork of
farm activity and family life.
Every domestic animal is
represented from horses, cows,
sheep, pigs, ducks, chickens,
and turkeys to dogs and cats.
Wild life was equally well-
portrayed: fox, deer, bear, coon,
beaver — even a few exotic
animals like a giraffe and lion,
perhaps indicating the the
circus came to town and
would probably date the quilt
ten years later. At the top is the
farm house and throughout
are shown people who were
probably family members:
children playing patticake, a boy
with his flail, a girl picking
apples, a man fiddling, another
whittling and probably
Mrs. Haskins herself working
on the quilt.

Blanket
1825
Polly Brown, Ira, Vermont
Wool
82½" x 83½"
Loaned by the
Vermont Historical Society

This blanket was woven
and embroidered by Polly
Brown for her daughter
Arethusa's trousseau. She
was married at sixteen to
John Williams.

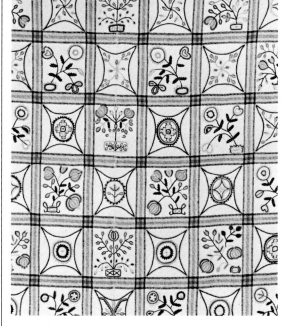

In recent years, though, lots of people have
come who do indeed have a shot at doing Vermont
stuff for themselves. Once again some of the
old hill farms resound to the cheerful tunk of the
axe getting up firewood and the dulcet squirting
of milk (often as not from a nanny goat) against
the pail. There is, in fact, a proliferating industry
geared to the greater satisfaction of this effort.
A cornucopia of aids for country living offers
books and magazines telling how to become
instant homesteaders: "new and improved" wood-
splitting devices which promise surcease from
the old splitting maul and wedge of my youth (and
aren't as quick or efficient); receipts for pickling
anything from beets to bears; instructions, tools
and even kits for building "authentic" Post and
Beam houses (with solar and a Commander to
pound in the pegs); and Country Store catalogs
selling a range of nineteenth century goods from
butter prints to well buckets. Most of the people
buying these delights work hard and their efforts
are creditable, for this is still a tough place in
which to make a living and people in ordinary
circumstances need to muster all of the ingenuity
of which they are capable.

The sober people who stare out at us so
quietly from old photographs do so from a firsthand acquaintance with life in a culture of extreme
scarcity of means. Between their lives and ours
lies an abyss of unshared and unknowable experience of life. There is a difference of magnitude
to living in a place and time in which substantial
numbers of girls and boys cannot be sent to school
beyond the sixth or eighth grades; in a partly
barter economy which provides no money cushion
between making it or not making it; where the long
daily round on a farm or in a village mill offers
not much more than simple survival.

What factors gave form and coherence to the strongly identifiable Vermont folk culture of the nineteenth and early twentieth centuries?

First is the fact of late settlement by a homogeneous population of ninety percent English stock in the most mountainous state in the Union. Vermont was not settled until the end of the French and Indian Wars in 1760 — one hundred fifty years after the rest of New England. Vermont was the first American frontier after initial settlement. The patterns of life first brought here were traditional English ones marked with the imprint of one hundred fifty years of adaptation to life along the Atlantic Seaboard.

Within the prolonged isolation and harsh climate of mountainous Vermont frontier settlements, old ways endured for much longer than in the rest of New England. And it should not be forgotten that as a legacy from the New Hampshire Grants period of its existence Vermont was, from 1777 to 1791, for fourteen years a republic completely independent from the United States. As a republic the state made its laws, minted its coinage and acted as a sovereign nation. These factors, in combination with a loose settlement pattern of scattered farms instead of the tight village clusters of southern New England, account for the persistence of a frontier cast of mind well into the twentieth century. They have strongly influenced the cultural patterns and outlook which still flourish among Vermonters today.

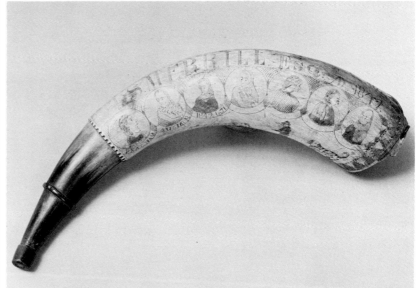

82.

Needlepoint Rug
c. 1810
Anna Baker,
Bakersfield, Vermont
Wool on linen with
bamboo stitch
60" L x 25" W
Loaned by the
Shelburne Museum

Anna Baker was a member of
the Baker family who founded
Bakersfield. According to
family tradition she may have
made the rug as early as 1790.

Powder Horn
1847
S. Merrill (possibly Samuel
b. 1792) Peacham, Vermont
Horn
3½" H x 14" L x 3" Diam.
Loaned by Hillary Underwood

Merrill has carved portraits
of himself, his wife and five
children on his horn. Below
these he depicts different family
members doing various farm
chores.

Vermonters offer almost a laboratory example
of a traditional pre-industrial culture as it came to
grips with the post-Industrial Revolution between
1870 and 1930. Their tenaciousness and rural
ingenuity made **selective** use of a small number
of artifacts from the many spewed out by the
emergent factory system developing in the urban
areas of the country. In so doing, these people
bent new implements and devices to their own use
and not the other way round! For the rest of their
needs they retained their almost fierce sense
of independence of the outside world in doing for
themselves or doing without.

Vermont farmers and villagers continued
through the 1930's to live within the bounds of
a subsistence-oriented culture. They relied upon
small village mills, draft animals, simple tools
and human muscle to furnish the daily needs of
life. For most of this time, "oxen ruled the world."
Hand tools and methods for sowing seed, cul-
tivating corn, cradling and binding wheat and
oats, digging potatoes, threshing and winnowing
grain and building fence all persisted on Vermont
hill farms side by side with new inventions.

By the 1890's the Vermont countryside
appeared quite different from what it is today.
The land then was seventy-five percent cleared,
with twenty-five percent in woods; today it is just
the reverse. As a state we're going back to woods.
Farms, back then, ran seventy to a hundred acres
divided into tillage, mowing, pasture and woodlot.
Buildings — and I commend to your attention
the purity of line and volume of old Vermont
houses and barns — centered on the barnyard,
where fifteen or twenty cows and perhaps some
sheep could take exercise and water in the winter.

The house and outsheds often were connected
to the barn. Known as continuous architecture,
this line of buildings formed a windbreak, kept
everything under cover, eliminated going out
into the snow to do barn work and saved labor and
material by leaving out unnecessary walls. Most
farms had an ice house, smoke house, corn crib,
tool sheds and workshop. It is little realized today
how many of these disappeared shortly after the
advent of electricity on the farm. Farms now
present a very different appearance from what
they did even as late as the 1920's.

Villages, too, have seen their share of change.
The livery stable and blacksmith shop are gone.
A few old country stores hang on. But the greatest
change lies in the hundreds of village mills and
shops which have vanished almost without
exception. These tiny water-powered industries
made Vermont all but independent of urban areas
to the south. Some of the mill men, like the hill
farmers, hung on for a surprisingly long time —
just too stubborn to quit, I guess, and I'm grateful
I've been privileged to know some of both.

I'd have to say I believe that those born not
much after 1900 were the very last generation to
know the old rural culture whose roots clearly
lay in medieval times. Self-sufficiency and traditional lore were the lodestones of their lives. Today
our lives rest on industrial techniques based
upon the machine. Our knowledge of the lives of
our fathers and grandfathers lies, now, in oral
tradition. Not many years hence, even this voice
will be stilled. Nothing will be left to bridge the
gap to an utterly different way of life from which
we come.

"…the stentorian cries of 'haw, haw' and 'gee,
gee' which once resounded on almost every
farmstead have fallen into unanswering silence."[1]

[1]Jared van Wagenen, Jr., **The Golden Age of Homespun** (New York:
Hill and Wang, 1963), p. 48.

84.

Chain Saw Farmer
1976
Frank Patoine, Walden, Vermont
Pine, painted
7'4" H x 10" W
Loaned by Frank Patoine

From Generation to Generation

Rosa Patoine was born in Brompton, Quebec and moved to Vermont when she was seventeen in November 1924. Her mother's brother had encouraged their whole family to come to Vermont, where prices were cheaper, to buy a farm. Her father went with his brother-in-law and "things looked so good" he bought a farm in South Walden. The move was not popular with his family.

"It was a sad beginning. The house was cold. We had few necessities. There were two stoves, two beds, a table and a few chairs. There was much snow and we had to walk most of the time. Nevertheless we settled in — Father, Mother, and we three girls. After the good times we shared in Canada, this was a strange place to us. We had only one French-speaking neighbor.

But before long Rosa had adjusted well, learned English and married Henri Patoine (who spoke very little French). With him she had sixteen children and worked on the farm. Life was hard; they had no running water, no central heating, no electricity and no tractor. There were also two disastrous fires. Despite these hardships, Mrs. Patoine tried to raise all her children "as God would have wanted me to," making all their clothes and household furnishings by hand.

Through her creativity — using and re-using everything around her — and her fine handiwork, the Patoine home was brightened by color and pattern. From grain bags, well bleached and sewn together, she made a coverlet decorated with the military insignias of her son and one or two nephews and cousins. From worn out farm clothes, she made braided rugs or hooked patterns over burlap. Quilts, curtains, children's clothing — she made everything with an artistic flair, and all by hand. It wasn't until 1946, when her oldest son put electricity into the house that she had a sewing machine, given her by her second son.

Today Mrs. Patoine still creates artistically from what she has around her. One unusual item Mrs. Patoine made was a rug braided from five hundred forty-five plastic bread bags, which she saved while she was working as a cook for a day care center. She was so successful at blending the colors that she won first prize with her creation at the Caledonia County Fair in 1979.

Often in a family this artistic expression is fostered, passed down, generation after generation. It may take a different form, but it is still recognizable. Frank, Rosa's ninth child, seems to have inherited this trait. "Francis had a talent for drawing, even at the age of four." As he says "I always was interested in animals, so Mom would cut them out with her scissors and I'd fool with them." It wasn't long before he was carving out animals with his jack knife. "I was always puttering around with a jack knife." Animals, airplanes, sailboats — whatever caught his fancy. Frank's interest in animals has never ceased and today he makes his living where he is most at home, in the woods, logging, trapping or hunting. His carvings reflect his interest — deer, bear, duck.

One day, he substituted his chain saw for his jack knife and carved out a tall, droopily-mustachioed farmer. He'd had a number of logs which he used to practice on with his axes and saws for the lumber jack contest. But one pine log he had never touched. "It had just laid there for a couple of years. And well, I took my chain saw and just started whacking away at it and that's what I got. I did use the chisel a little bit around the face, smoothed it up a little." Frank enjoys using different materials and with his interest in hunting, it is not surprising that he has also tried his talents on decorating powder horns in traditional scrimshaw fashion. According to Frank, he is not the only one to have inherited his mother's abilities. He has one or two nephews and nieces interested in both sculpting and painting. It remains to be seen if the talents will be fostered in a traditional direction. ●

Bread Bag Rug
1978
Rosa Patoine,
Hardwick, Vermont
Plastic bread bags
73″ x 54″
Loaned by Rosa Patoine

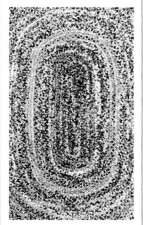

Bluebill Duck Decoy
1978
Frank Patoine, Walden, Vermont
Pine, painted
7½″ H x 15″ L x 6″ W
Loaned by Frank Patoine

An excellent trapper and hunter, it is only natural that Frank should try his hand at carving decoys. This is one of his first. Since that time he has carved several more.

Powder Horn
1968
Frank Patoine, Walden, Vermont
Steer horn
11½″ L x 3″ Diam.
Loaned by Frank Patoine

Like most scrimshaw, this carving was not done at home. Frank carved this one in Haines, Alaska. However, the map depicted on the horn is the area of East Hardwick where Frank lives.

Grainbag Coverlet
1967
Rosa Patoine,
Hardwick, Vermont
Cotton
95″ x 65″
Loaned by Rosa Patoine

Canes

Snake Cane
1927
Kenneth Larrow,
Pittsford, Vermont
Wood, painted
36″ L x 1¼″ Diam. Head: 4¼″ L
Loaned by Gregg Blasdel

This cane was made by Larrow for his father when he was undergoing treatment for tuberculosis at the Vermont Sanatorium in Pittsford.

Woodpecker Cane
Early 20th century
Artist unknown, Vermont
Wood (spruce), painted
34″ L x 1½″ Diam. Head: 4¼″ L
Loaned by Gregg Blasdel

Cane
c. 1960
Charles E. Chaffee,
Sutton, Vermont
Wood (spruce)
34½″ L x 1¼″ Diam.
Private collection

When he worked in the woods Charles Chaffee used to select saplings with burls, cut them, bring them home and work them into canes. He carved all kinds of features to fit the particular burl— horses, Indian heads, and in this case "a fat human being."

The cane is a popular item in folk art. Vermonters are often in the woods and frequently pick out naturally shaped canes in their wanderings. Some of these are left in their natural state, but a great many more are carved and decorated in quiet moments for use by family members and friends. ●

"One for the Crow..."

"Say I hired somebody to help me plant my corn. You marked it all out. You couldn't do anything else, by golly, you marked it out by hand. I was thinking about it the other night. We used to say,

One for the blackbird,
One for the crow.
One for the cutworm
And four to grow.

So they'd put seven kernels in a hill. Figured three of them would be destroyed before maturity. So they get four, four stalks of corn. And years ago — I've heard this many a time — had a fellow who couldn't count. And to make it easier for him they'd take a T.D. pipe. You know, one of those clay pipes. And they'd put some butternut leaves down the bottom of the bowl so it would hold just seven kernels. Just scoop up that bowl full of corn and drop it. Move on to the next place. Man comes along with a hoe and covers it."

Farmer
Sixty-six years of age
North Thetford, Vermont

"We owned a big wood lot up on the mountain. Three miles away. There's a foot path up over that mountain. I walked up there those two winters and there wasn't anybody within miles of me. Some days my father come up and helped me; some days he wouldn't. Take my dog with me. I built a shelter up there out of old boards and a little old roofing and spruce boughs where I could build a fire and eat my dinner. I went up there and chopped cordwood all day and I got up there by nine in the morning and I left when the stars were starting to shine at night. And back up the next morning. Draw the wood home. Pile it up right out here and saw it up with a gasoline engine and a sawing machine and split it. Deliver it to the village in a dump cart for ten dollars a cord. You couldn't get one more cent if you tried, to save your soul."

Farmer
Sixty-six years of age
North Thetford, Vermont

"I was my father's hired man. He'd rather have me. I had two brothers and he'd rather have me outdoors with him or doing things because he said I did it as he wanted me to. So I was his hired help. And yet we had our chores in the house too. We went to school and when we came home we had our chores to do before anything else.

"We had to fill the wood box. And that wasn't a boy's job. That was our job because the boys were outdoors working. So we had our wood box to keep filled. We had our dishes to do. We had to bring up so many potatoes and wash 'em and keep ready for the next meal. And vegetables from down cellar so that my mother wouldn't have to go down and get them. She had a lot to do."

Farm woman
Born 1885
Sharon and East Barnard, Vermont

Carved Corner Post
c. 1875
Russell Risley, Kirby, Vermont
Wood
47½″ H x 7½″ Diam.
Loaned by Thomas E. Hannan

Russell Risley (1842-1927) spent all but his last few years on his family's farm in Kirby. There he peopled the outdoors as well as the interior of his house with paintings and carvings. Even the dasher on his handmade broad-runner sleigh was painted inside and out with local landscapes. He carved his fence posts and granite rocks. As one neighbor remembers, when she was a child

"We loved to see the funny-looking wooden faces and animals he had carved out of blocks of wood. Sometimes we even saw him carving out a face with his sharp axe. The pictures on the barn always fascinated us, because some of them were of people we knew. For a long time there was a picture of a shapely young woman in the nude painted on the barn that we stole furtive, embarrassed glances at whenever we could. We had heard our parents talk about that picture. They thought it was a disgrace for an old bachelor like Mr. Risley to paint anything like that right on the outside of his barn!"
(Toussaint, p. 113)

"...they used to lay over up here and boom the logs up there to Wells River. The men would hit the town, by gorry, and have a hell of a spree. Some of them wound up down there at the County Farm up there to Haverhill, if they got too boisterous. And work out their fines. Oh it used to be, used to be quite a hilarious town up there, I guess on both sides of the river in days gone by."

Farmer
Sixty-six years of age
North Thetford, Vermont

"Oh, I was eleven years old. Working out and they had a horse there, honest to God, it was as big as an elephant. A foot ruler would measure him crossways he was so thin. I took pretty good care of him but, boy, you'd go in aside of him and his eyes would be rolling. I'd land clear across the barn. But Dad showed me how to go in beside a horse that kicks, so I wouldn't get hurt. You speak to him, pat him on the rump and crowd right in just as close to him as you can get. And then if they do kick, instead of getting you with a foot they hit you with their knees, you see. They don't have time to get the foot straightened out to hit you. I'd pick myself up and go right back in. I wouldn't do it today for a thousand dollars."

**Farmer, Mill worker,
Drummer**
Born 1903
McIndoe Falls, Vermont

90.

Birth-Death Records

There appears to have been an artist who worked in northern Vermont between 1820 and 1850 and who painted family records. The above are two examples. The artist is recognized by his heart and hand motifs. These family records are very different from the Frakturs of the Pennsylvania Germans which were closely tied to their religious beliefs.

Wright Family Record
c. 1820-49
Artist unknown, Montpelier, Vermont
Watercolor on paper
9″ H x 14″ W
Loaned by the Vermont Historical Society

Bliss Family Record
Between 1827-42
Artist unknown, Colchester, Vermont
Watercolor on paper
13″ H x 18″ W
Private collection

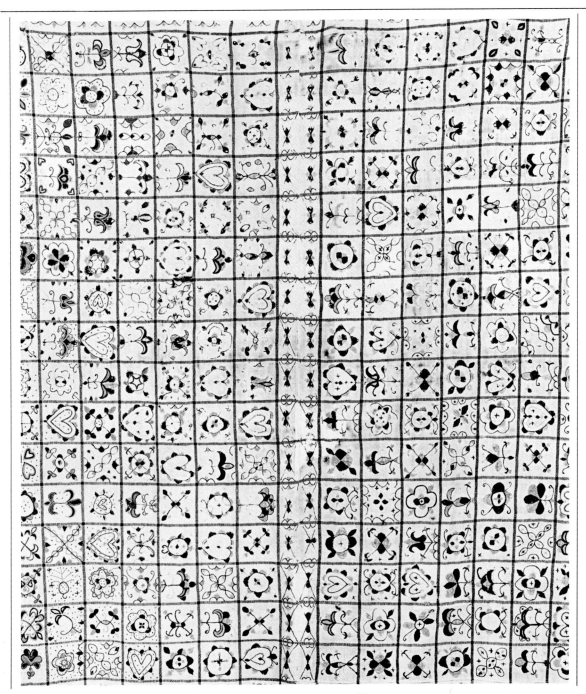

Coverlet
Early 1800's
Elizabeth Meigs Chittenden,
Williston, Vermont
Wool
82½" x 78½"
Loaned by the
Vermont Historical Society

This coverlet was made by
Elizabeth Meigs Chittenden
(Mrs. Thomas) for her daughter
Betsy, who married James Hill,
an early settler of Charlotte.
The wool for this spread was
raised on the Chittenden's
farm in Williston, and was spun
by Mrs. Chittenden.

Coverlet
Early 1800's
Unknown, Vermont
Wool
90½" x 91½"
Loaned by the
Vermont Historical Society
  Handwoven wool and
then embroidered with dark
blue (indigo-dyed) wool.

Bed Rug
1805
Rachel Packard,
Jericho, Vermont
Wool
93½" x 90"
Collections of Greenfield Village
and the Henry Ford Museum,
Dearborn, Michigan

Bed rugs have been made
and used in Vermont since at
least 1779. These rugs, usually
initialed and dated by their
makers were mostly made with
hand-spun wool and were
used as coverlets for the bed,
rather than for the floor.

Caswell Carpet
1832-35
Zeruah Higley Guernsey
Caswell (Mrs. Memri Caswell),
Castleton, Vermont
Home-dyed yarn
13½' x 12'
Photograph courtesy of the
Metropolitan Museum of Art

When Zeruah was sixteen
her father whittled a wooden
hook for her. By the time she was
twenty-five she was accomplished in the needle arts and
when her father gave her a lamb,
she sheared it, carded and
spun the wool, dyed it, and wove
the coarse homespun that was
used as the foundation for
her embroidery. She then drew
on her design and chain-
stitched it, embroidering each
block separately and then
sewing the pieces together. It
is said that two Potawatomi
Indians who were students
at Castleton and boarded at the
Guernsey's for a month, each
drew a block which she then
embroidered. Their initials
remain, F. B. and L. F. M., as a
permanent reminder.

The carpet took two or three
years to complete and when
finished contained a removable
embroidered panel used to
cover the hearth in the summer.

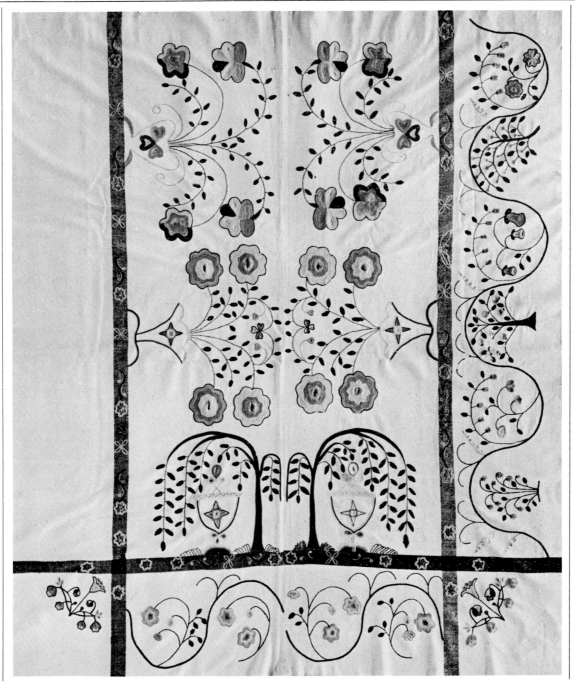

Blanket
1827
Syrena Scott Parmelee,
Bristol, Vermont
Wool
80" x 88"
Loaned by the
Vermont Historical Society

Made by a sixteen year old girl, this blanket was first woven from homespun wool. With brightly colored handspun yarn, she then embroidered the tree of life design, so popular on New England gravestones, combining it with the basket pattern.

Maple Sugar Molds

Most of the early sugar molds were hand carved. Later these were supplanted by tin molds. Before white sugar could be obtained easily and cheaply, maple sugar was used as a substitute on most Vermont farms. This sugar was usually put down into tubs in syrup form and when it crystallized was used as a sugar substitute. Hand carved molds were made for "sugar cakes" which would be used for home consumption or perhaps sold at the local general store or shipped out of state. One woman remembers how sixty years ago,

"Mother used to make all the sugar cakes on our kitchen stove over a very hot fire. She had a big old square iron pan that took the full top of the stove. And she had to cook the syrup to a certain consistency (I never recall that she used a thermometer). She made perfect maple sugar cakes. And then they were poured into these sugar molds, and then they were taken out very carefully. We weren't allowed to do that. We'd break the cakes. Mother used to do it. And then we used to pack those very carefully and ship them out." ●

Cap Wilcox was born in 1873 in Victory and died in 1970. He was a harness maker by trade but had been interested in whittling and woodworking throughout his life. It was after he retired in his early seventies that he began carving in earnest. Because he was a harness maker and had a great love of horses, these were his first subjects — complete with saddles and bridles. He also carved a number of steer and oxen. It is said that he would look at a piece of wood until he saw the animal in it and then "just carve the rest away." (Finn, **Vermont Life**, 1950, p. 43)

Chair
c. 1880-1890
Ebenezer P. Colton,
Irasburg, Vermont
Maple
35½″ H x 24″ W x 20″ D
Loaned by Clare Phillips

Colton discovered that a vine growing around a young maple would leave an indentation. With an artistic eye toward the future, he went out "where the maples were thick" and twisted the vine "as tight as he could" around a couple of maples about a half inch in diameter. Ten years later he returned, cut the trees, and from them made two identical chairs.

Rocking Chair - Cradle - Loveseat
c. 1820
Edward Hatch,
Wardsboro, Vermont
Wood, painted
As cradle: 29″ H x 31″ L
As rocker: 40″ H x 21″ W
Loaned by the Farrar-Mansur House Museum

This is an original piece of furniture invented and made by Edward Hatch. It was used interchangeably as a rocking chair, cradle, or loveseat with a removable comb back to be used as a guard rail for the cradle or as a head rest for the rocking chair. The seat and left arm rest are also moveable. By 1850 this unique piece of furniture had been patented. The Sheldon Museum has a later example.

"...if we started to school and they said the drive was in, we never went to school. We went to the drive. Sometimes they'd be there 2 weeks and we would spend most of the two weeks up to the drive. They had lard come five pound pails... We would get a couple pails of beans — a pail of hard boiled eggs. I've seen them time after time, day after day just to go out on the lunch wagon, thirty cases of eggs, thirty dozen in a case."

Farmer, Mill worker, Drummer
Born 1903
McIndoe Falls, Vermont

"Boys always slept upstairs and upstairs in most houses, old houses, never was finished off. There was open chambers. And sometimes there was cracks. I've heard my Dad tell about how sometimes he'd wake up in the morning and the snow would be on his bed. But I don't know, they never had boys sleep in a warm room. I don't know why but they never did.

"My great grandmother, she used to have-herbs and roots and barks and I don't know what in this big open chamber. All the rafters was hanging with things drying.

"Neighbors used to be neighborly. You was all the time having somebody run in you know. And help each other and if one person went to town, why they got the mail for all the folks there was. Cause there was no rural free delivery then. And so you never knew when somebody might be running in or somebody happened to be sick why you went to help them."

Farm woman
Born 1889
Barnard, Vermont

"In the ell part there was a summer kitchen. And there was a great big cupboard. It was the whole height of the room. And big doors, two doors that opened all the way to the floor. And grandmother made cheese just like the big wheels you can get in the store. She made pretty good wheel cheese that summer. She had to grease them with pork fat so's they wouldn't crack open. And you'd have to turn them after you got them in the cupboard. Well there was three or four big cheeses in there, enough to last a whole year. Then she'd make up a mess of pies when the apples was good and mincemeat and all this, that and the other. And she always had pies on hand. Those shelves would be all pies, you know. They'd freeze in the winter.

"And Dad used to keep pigs. And they'd take all the fresh pork and the loins and the roasts and things like that. Freeze them and wrap them in paper and pack them in a big barrel and poke in oats all round. Oats somehow or other, I don't know why, but they seem to be colder than anything else. When you'd have a warm spell in the winter time they wouldn't thaw out — not ordinarily you know."

Farm woman
Born 1889
Barnard, Vermont

"He used to come here and work for a while. Sometimes he would be here for a few months. Other times it would be a very short time. You'd wake up in the morning, he'd be gone. When his star moved, he moved. That's why he left, because his star had moved and he'd be gone. He'd never say goodbye or anything else to anybody. He'd just take off — next thing you know he'd be back here again — might be a year or two."

Farmer
Sixty years of age
Hartland, Vermont

Whimsey Toy
c. 1890
Henry Cox, Monkton, Vermont
Carved wood and wire
20" H x 1½" W
Loaned by Louie and
Rita Masso

Henry Cox was a trapper and logger but in his spare time he used to carve. This whimsey toy is a well used example. He also was known to carve canes and rings.

Page's Box Shop
William, Charles and Frank Page of Page's Box Shop, East Corinth, Vermont. The present operator, Maurice Page, is the fourth generation to own and operate the shop. Mr. Page works daily making water tubs and boxes. Hundreds of small mills like this one furnished most of the daily needs of Vermonters.
Courtesy Maurice Page, family collection

Oliver A. Hastings
McIndoe Falls, Vermont
Farmer, master carpenter and mason, Connecticut River log driver. Most Vermonters were able to turn their hand to anything.
Courtesy Scott Hastings, Sr., family collection

Horse, Sulky and Driver
c. 1955
Herbert "Cap" Wilcox, St. Johnsbury, Vermont
Wood
5½" H x 14" L x 6" W
Loaned by Mrs. Howard Farmer
This horse and sulky Cap Wilcox carved for his friend Howard Farmer, with whom he shared a mutual love of harness racing. Wilcox always felt that this was one of his best carvings.

"Drop the Handkerchief"
1979
Lee Hull,
South Royalton, Vermont
Oil painting
21½" H x 27½" L
Loaned by Lee Hull

As Lee Hull describes it, "Back in 1910 in North Fairfield there was no electricity and no television. In the evenings we used to get together and have a lawn party and play drop the handkerchief."

"This Joe Blair — I was thirteen years old, and I went up there for spring vacation and worked for him. Used to have a month or six weeks in spring that they'd close the school right down and they called it spring vacation. He come up one night about eleven o'clock and woke me. Said Phelps had some new horses in from the West and he wanted me to take the old team down and pick a new one and bring them home. And I said, 'I don't know anything about it.' All he said was 'you go down, I have told Phelps to let you have any team you pick out.' Well, I was down there at six-thirty the next morning and they had sixty horses and I looked at every one at least three times.

"And D.G., he was a local character, started hollering and telling me what to get for a pair of horses. Said, 'I don't know why they send a God damn kid down — he don't know anything about horses.' Phelps heard him and he said 'I don't care if he wants to look at them ten times apiece, you keep showing them till he makes up his mind. You understand that he's only a young boy, and this man is going to pay for this pair of horses, has got enough faith in his judgment about horses so that he sent him down here to pick the team instead of coming himself. I finally made up my mind — there was a pair of stripe faced bays with four white feet, Clydesdales. Big, rangy fellows but they were a nice team. And I said, 'I am going to take this team.'

"And this D. G. said, 'Jesus Christ that shows how much you know about horses on a farm around here, long legged horses like that.'

"I said, 'I'll take that team and you help me get the harnesses on them.'

"Phelps come in and he said, 'Got them picked out?' And I said, 'That one, that team of rangy stripe face bays.'

"He says, 'You made a damn good choice, that's as good a team as there is in the barn.' And he says, 'I don't know whether you can handle that pair of horses or not.'

"I said, 'You help me get them hitched up to that pung sled and headed toward the farm and don't you worry about it.' So he did and Phelps said, 'D.G. you hitch up my driving horse. I'm going to follow along behind and see he's all right.'

"Well we hitched them up in the barnyard and when they went out the sled brushed the gate on both sides it was flopping so and they were right in a dead run. I had two sharp corners to make and I bet that sled went sideways twenty feet on each one. And then I had five miles straight up hill. I had a nice whip and I put it right to them.

"Phelps was trying to keep up. The first pitch I come to they was lagging, don't you think they weren't, so I stopped them. I hung onto the reins but I got right out and got hold of the bridles and talked to them…and Phelps come along and he seen I was resting them and breathing them and not going to hurt them any. He says, 'You know this is a fool's errand I'm on. I'm going to turn round and go home. You're all right.' And he told Joe, 'You know something, that kid picked out the best team of horses there was in that bunch.' But I'd already had a lot of experience with horses with Dad you know."

Farmer, Mill worker, Drummer
Born 1903
McIndoe Falls, Vermont

Scott E. Hastings, Jr.
Director,
Billings Farm Museum

Rural Occupations:
Off the Farm

Off the Farm

In nineteenth century Vermont, the most rural of rural states, the popular expectation would be that everyone not living in one of the larger population centers was a farmer, or, at the very least, engaged in some kind of agricultural activity. Literally what else was there to do in a state that largely ignored the urban industrial revolution and boasted for decades of having more cows than people?

Farmers there were aplenty, but in the mid-nineteenth century, as is equally true today, there were a number of rural occupations which existed in support of agricultural enterprise, as well as ministers and teachers who helped keep the social fabric intact. In addition, the developing of mining, quarrying, and stone preparation — in short, the extractive industries — offered welcome employment off the farm.

Some farm families found rural avocations that could be pursued in quiet seasons, thus illustrating the difficulty of making a sharp distinction among farm and other rural occupations. One example is basket making. While some families produced baskets for a living, often the farmer's family would plan to make a few brown ash baskets or cane a few chairs during the winter months.

Vermonters were also travelers, though that is not the role in which they are familiarly perceived. The great waves of emigration from Vermont to the welcoming West began early in the nineteenth century and continued for decades. The thousands of Vermont men and boys who answered Father Abraham's call to preserve the Union in the 1860's learned firsthand that there was another world beyond Vermont's borders. Many veterans returned home simply to say goodbye and gather their belongings before setting out for new homes in other parts of the nation. Others returned to their hill farms with widened personal horizons; travel for them could now be seen as acceptable, perhaps desirable. Maybe this explains in part why one out of every six Vermonters visited the Centennial Exposition in Philadelphia in 1876.

We are so used to celebrating Vermont's contribution to western expansion that we forget that some Vermonters looked steadily eastward. For some landlocked Vermonters the lure of the sea was strong; here was adventure and opportunity to match the excitement of Indian fighting and frontier life. From New England's harbors vessels still sailed in search of whales, carried northern ice to equatorial nations, or freighted up with cargo and passengers to go around the Horn, perhaps in search of California gold.

The long sea voyages left sailors with time on their hands, time frequently spent in the carving of scrimshaw to delight the folks at home or to sell at ports of call along the way. Artistically untutored, the sailors developed their own unique patterns and styles. Here and there a sailor would even try his hand at painting.

Scrimshaw Cane
1852
H. J. West, Vermont
Narwhal tusk
36″ L x 1″ Diam.
Loaned by Green Mountain Antiques

Scrimshaw
1861
James Hamilton,
Barre, Vermont
Whale's tooth
4⅝″ L x 1⅝″ Diam.
Loaned by the Vermont Historical Society

James Hamilton was master of the "Charles W. Morgan" on her sixth voyage, begun October 4, 1859 and concluded May 12, 1863 in New Bedford, Massachusetts. On this voyage she hunted whales along the west coast of South America, around Hawaii to the Okhotsk Sea and returned with a record cargo. Hamilton's journal is filled with references to his wife, Augusta, at home in Vermont, and on the date inscribed on the piece of scrimshaw which depicts "Home in Barre," "The ship was at anchor and the crew was employed in bringing aboard wood and cleaning below decks." This piece is interesting because scrimshaw is usually thought to be done by crew members rather than the captain of a whaling vessel.

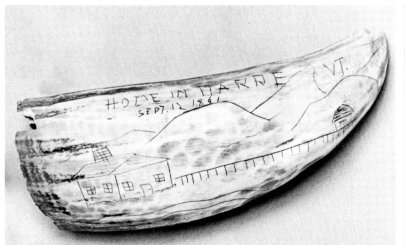

Schooner Weathervane
c. 1815
Unknown Portuguese man,
Weathersfield, Vermont
Wood, wire
64″ H x 75″ L
Loaned by the Vermont
Historical Society

This was made by a
"homesick Portuguese" who
worked on William C. Jarvis'
farm in Weathersfield. Jarvis
had been consul to Portugal and
was also responsible for
introducing Merino sheep
into Vermont.

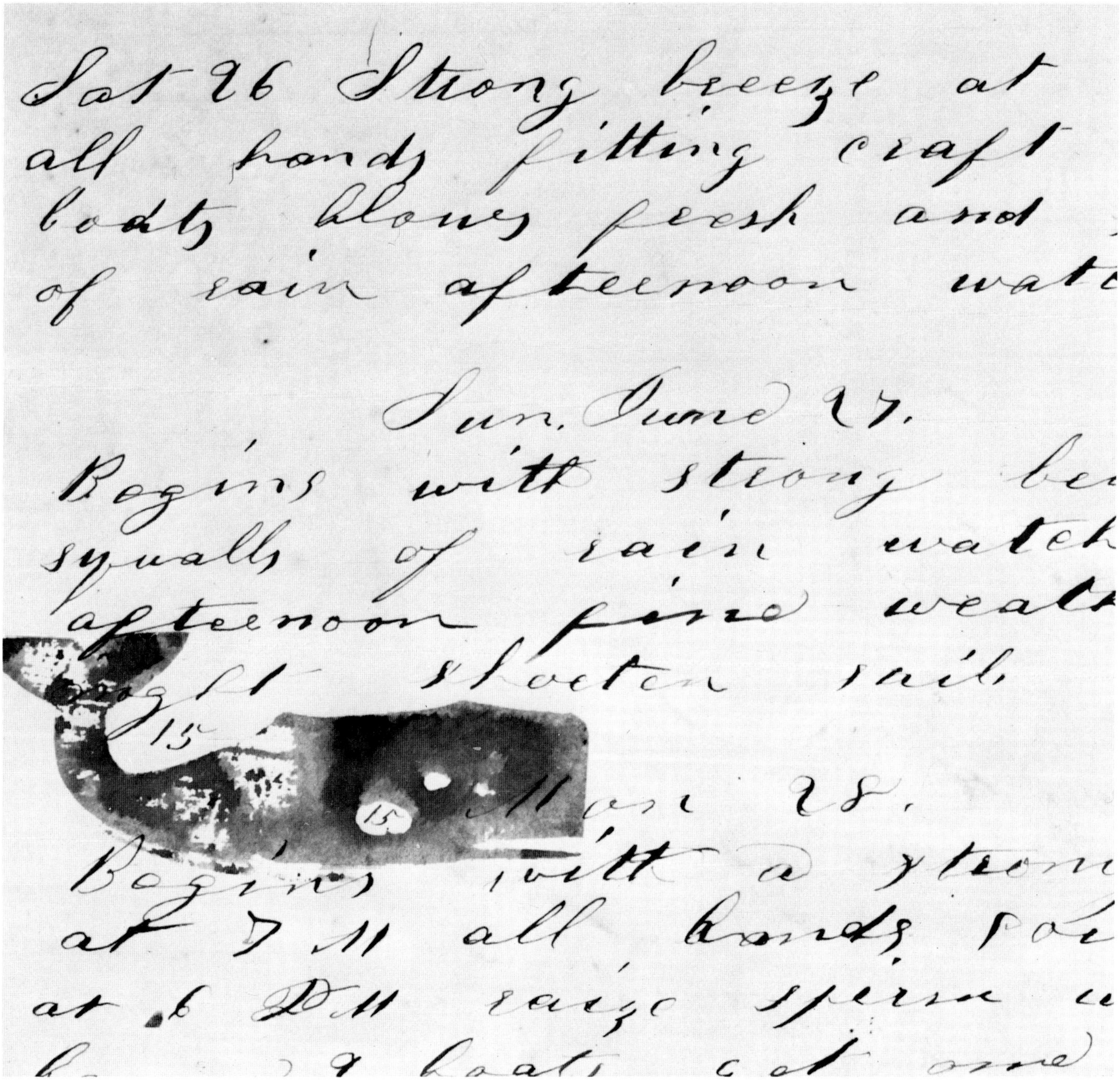

Sat 26 Strong breeze at
all hands fitting craft
boats blows fresh and
of rain afternoon watc

Sun June 27.
Begins with strong bre
squalls of rain watch
afternoon fine weath
ught shorten sail

15

15   Mon 28.
Begins with a xtreme
at 7 M all hands sou
at 6 PM raise sperm w
b   & boats cut one

Whaling Log
c. 1860
Nathaniel Burbank,
South Walden, Vermont
Paper and ink
13½" H x 8½" L
Loaned by Mrs. Pauline Welch

Nathaniel Burbank

When he was in his twenties, Nathaniel Burbank left his father's farm in South Walden to go whaling. He made three voyages, his first being on the bark "Joseph Grinnell" which went out to the Pacific and did not return for a good three and one-half years. It was on this voyage that he kept a journal using the "lost" whale stamp in an interesting geometric pattern. When a whale was harpooned, but lost, a stamp with a whale's tail was entered into the ship's log. When a whale was successfully taken, the whole whale was stamped in the log.

The watercolor of a harpooned whale and the two scrimshaw awls were also made by Burbank on this voyage. It wasn't until after the Civil War that Burbank returned to Walden, bought a farm and left the sea behind him.

●

Harpooned Whale
c. 1860
Nathaniel Burbank,
South Walden, Vermont
Watercolor
7½" H x 12⅞" L
Loaned by Mrs. Pauline Welch

Scrimshaw Awls
c. 1860
Whale's tooth
2⅝" L x ⅞" H x 3/16" D
(with hole)
3¾" L x ½" H x 5/16" D
(without hole)
Loaned by Mrs. Pauline Welch

Nathaniel Burbank and Family
Walden, Vermont

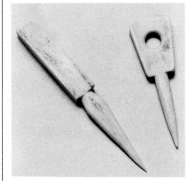

Horse Powered Saw
c. 1950
Burleigh Woodard,
West Charleston, Vermont
Wood
10″ H x 12½″ L x 12½″ W
Loaned by the Old Stone
House Museum

Burleigh Woodard (1895-1966) was born in Barton, and most of his working life was spent in the nearby towns of West Charleston and Glover as a teamster and a logger. He was always known for his fine teams and in the 1950's when poor health and age caught up with him, he turned to carving teams of horses working in all the capacities with which he had been so familiar.

Crown of Thorns
Picture Frame
1923-24
Maurice Wheeler,
Cabot, Vermont
Cedar
14½″ H x 10½″ W
Private collection

Maurice Wheeler, seen in the photograph, spent the fall and winter of 1923 and 1924 working in a logging camp in Berlin, New Hampshire. It was there he learned from a Russian logger how to carve the cedar pieces and then put them together so that they would interlock and hold.

Chain
1980
William Forbes,
Danville, Vermont
Wood
12′
Loaned by Edmond Menard

Since his retirement, William Forbes spends his time in woodworking and whittling. The chain is a common whittling motif, carved from a solid piece of wood.

Many farmers would cut enough logs each winter so that the farm needs for lumber could be met. A few farmers might run a trapline during the winter when the normal demands of the farm were lighter. The majority of the logging and trapping, however, was done by men who were specialists and virtually fulltime workers at their trade.

Even before the coming of the railroads the great log drives on the Connecticut and the heavy shipping of lumber north on Lake Champlain to Canada testified to an insatiable demand for lumber as the nations developed. With the perfecting of the sulphide process in paper manufacture, the demand for pulpwood grew. Armed only with an axe and crosscut saw, dependent upon horses or oxen to skid logs and finally draw them off to the sawmill, the logger worked long hours in all kinds of weather. Life in a logging camp, especially in winter, spawned folklore, songs, and sometimes unique wood carvings. It also brought on disagreements, fights, competitive feats of strength, and huge appetites. The whole tenor of camp life revolved around the excellence of the "cookee." If the "grub" was good, the men were happier and more productive. If it was less than good, the hard-working crew became irritable and eventually might drift off to other camps with better culinary reputations.

Sawmills and loggers complemented each other. Each community had at least one mill, though many had several. Here then was yet another rural occupation, the sawyer. It was he who would decide just how a log should be cut to produce the most and best lumber. He, too, would sharpen the saws and keep the machinery in operating order while his less skilled helpers handled logs and stacked lumber.

112.

Spruce Gum Boxes

It is believed that these items had their origin in the logging camps between 1880 and 1920. Generally they were made for wife or sweetheart and held a present of spruce gum. The boxes were often in the shape of books, hollowed in the center for the gum, with one end fitted with a slide. They have been commonly found in Maine, New Brunswick and New Hampshire, and now Vermont. (Dennis, pp. 20-21)

Spruce Gum Box
c. 1890-1910
Artist unknown, Vermont
Birch with cherry inlays
4¾" H x 3 1/16" W x
1 3/16" D
Loaned by the Billings
Farm Museum
    The cross on the front
and the heart on the back are
typical designs carved on
gum boxes.

Spruce Gum Box
c. 1890-1910
Artist unknown, Vermont
Pine, painted
4½" H x 4⅜" W x 1½" D
Loaned by the Billings
Farm Museum

Spruce Gum Box
c. 1890-1910
Artist unknown, Vermont
Pine
6½" H x 5" W x 1⅝" D
Loaned by the Billings
Farm Museum
    This gum box is a good
example of chip carving.

Spruce Gum Box
c. 1890-1910
Artist unknown, Vermont
Pine
4 5/16" H x 2¾" W x
1 7/16" D
Loaned by the Billings
Farm Museum

River Log Drive
Long Log Drive on the
Connecticut River between
Wilder and White River
Junction, Vermont c. 1912
showing the Mary Anne
(Cook shack), bateaus and
horse raft.
Photograph courtesy of
John St. Croix,
Hartford, Vermont

Logging Collage
1980
Roland Rochette,
Greensboro Bend, Vermont
Paint, wood,
cedar sprigs, gravel
18″ H x 24″ W
Private collection
"I left my job with the Canadian
Pacific Railroad to go over to
New Brunswick where my wife's
folks was pioneers. And I
worked in the woods in a camp.
This picture is the story of
logging and that's where I learned
this thing. Them two guys go
out and cut the trees with the
double axe and the crosscut saw.
(There are more than two,
you see, but I couldn't put all
on the picture). This building—
some of them call it a hoble—
it's the horse barn. They had
many horses. And over here, it's
the camp where the woodsmen
lived. They got a kitchen and
a sleeping room where the men
stay. And over here, this little
feller, he's skidding logs to put
them over here in the yard. This
is a skidway—some of them
were as high as thirty feet. There
were probably a thousand
logs in that, but I couldn't put it
that big. In the spring they go
down the river to the sawmill. So
that's the story of the picture."

Hanging Cradle
1875
Martin L. Linfield,
Braintree, Vermont
Pine
26½″ H x 36″ L x 16″ W
Loaned by the
Shelburne Museum
This cradle was made by
Martin Linfield for his daughter,
Sarah Rebecca Linfield who
was born March 5, 1875.

Inn Sign
c. 1824
Possibly Sheldon Peck,
Shoreham, Vermont
Wood, painted
69½″ H x 39″ W
Loaned by Frederick Lapham III
The A. Smith Inn and Store
began operation in 1824 and
continued until the mid-1830's.
It was located in Addison,
just over the Bridport line. In
the late 1820's Sheldon Peck
was residing in Bridport and
there are certain stylistic
similarities in the painting and
facial coloration that suggest
he might be the artist.

The trapper tended to be a solitary rural worker with highly specialized skills. Frequently boasting real or pseudo-Indian ancestry, the trapper pitted his knowledge and cunning against that of the animal world. In the summer he would carefully prepare the scents for his trapline, often using secret recipes that had been handed down from father to son or obtained from a trusted colleague. As the state settled more people, open farming grew, forests were cut back to make way for even more fields and pastures, and the trapper found his quarry shrinking in numbers. Late years have seen new forest growth and the expansion of animal life, yet the skillful trappers now number but a few.

Undoubtedly one of the most important non-farm artisans was the village blacksmith. While some of the larger farms maintained their own forges to handle minor repair work, the village smithy always had all he could do. Keeping the community's horses and oxen shod was a major task, to say nothing of the constant stream of broken tools and machinery that found their way to his door for repair. On occasion, however, some especially skilled blacksmiths would find time to produce decorative ironwork that might range from fancy grills for the local bank's windows to delicate stands for my lady's inkwell. A good smithy could listen to his customer's wishes and quickly forge the desired part or tool without the necessity of blueprints. He was creative and usually profane, a romantic figure with tobacco juice on his chin, a magnet for the village children, and a source of moral concern to their mothers, yet without him no nineteenth century community could have existed.

Other crafts supported rural life. The tinsmith not only produced all kinds of house and kitchenware, he also fashioned the farmers' lanterns, pails, measures, scoops, and, of course, sap buckets.

The cooper made the barrels, the hogsheads, the cheese boxes, and the firkins while the wheelwright's special skill made wagons and carts possible. Others working with wood spanned a variety of skills. The general carpenter's work would vary from building houses and barns to making a new set of steps for the back porch.

Blacksmith
Photograph courtesy of the Vermont Historical Society

Blacksmith Sign
c. 1860
Artist unknown,
Newfane, Vermont
Wooden sign, painted
37″ H x 28″ W
Loaned by the Historical Society of Windham County
    This was the trade sign of Elihu Park, blacksmith in Newfane.

Tin Fiddle
c. 1908
Forrest A. "Strad" Gray,
East Calais, Vermont
Tin, painted
23½" L x 8" W x 1¼" D
Loaned by Forrest A. Gray

Strad Gray was born in Calais township in 1884 and grew up on a farm there. But he was not inclined toward farming, so his father hired him out, first to a druggist, and later to a tinsmith in Cabot. Tinsmithing became his profession.

As a child Strad learned to play the fiddle — restringing his grandfather's with fishline. One day when his boss was away, Gray, fed up with making heavy tin water pails, pulled out an outline of a fiddle that he'd "drawed out" and went to making this tin fiddle.

Today at 97 Strad is still best known for his fiddling and his tin fiddle. ("Oral History Project" **News and Notes** Vermont Historical Society Vol. 24, No. 2, 1973)

Tin Cradle
c. 1860-1875
Member of Young family,
Manchester, Vermont
Tin, painted, tole decoration,
wooden rockers
36" L x 24" W x 18½" D
Loaned by the Manchester
Historical Society

Young had a tinshop at Factory Point (Manchester Center) in 1871. He probably made the cradle for one of his own children as it was kept in the family until it was given to the Manchester Historical Society.

Whirligig
Early 20th century
Artist unknown,
St. Albans, Vermont
Painted tin, wire and metal rods
25" H x 33½" W
Loaned by Frederick and
Mary Fried

Whirligigs are popular in Vermont. This is unusual as it is made of tin; most are made of wood. Not only are whirligigs decorative but it is said that the noise they make keeps the moles away.

117.

Fireboard
c. 1795
Artist unknown,
Addison, Vermont
Wood, painted
2'10½" H x 3'8" W
Loaned by John Strong
Mansion, Vermont State
Society, D.A.R., Inc.

Fireboards, which were so common in the rest of New England, do not seem to have been as popular in Vermont. Perhaps this is because summer was so short. A common saying is that there are two seasons in Vermont: winter and the fourth of July. The vase of flowers depicted on the fireboard is a typical motif, for flowers would commonly be used as a fireplace decoration in the summer months.

The framer would put up the skeleton of a house or a barn, while the cabinet maker would build fine furniture for home or church or work with the wagonmaker in producing elegant carriages as well as more utilitarian farm wagons. Yet another woodworking specialist was the carver of butter molds. He would most commonly produce standard one-pound molds, but would happily make custom molds that carried the purchaser's initials or farm product. Hence Addison County butter molds might feature sheep while the maple leaf would be found throughout the state.

"Working out," meaning away from the home or farm, was not uncommon in rural or village life during the middle and late 1800's. In addition to the young men and women who, at least for a time, became hired men or hired girls, local civic, merchandising, or manufacturing enterprises offered other opportunities for "outside" employment. In addition to the teachers, the ministers, the doctors, and lawyers, others followed some perhaps less exalted work as seamstresses, boot and shoe makers, millers, workers at local creameries and cheese factories, machine tenders in the many small woolen and cotton mills, or clerks in the village or crossroads stores.

"Working out" became a real necessity in many cases. Farm cash income was usually small and frequently insufficient to meet even basic needs, especially if the family was large. If the farmer or one of his sons or daughters could "work out" in the mills, quarries, or offices, that supplemental cash income would be enough to sustain the farming operation. To this day there are still thousands of Vermonters who live in the country, where they maintain small or medium sized farming operations, while earning their livings in off-farm employment.

Vermont's abundant geological resources provided a variety of non-farm occupations in many different parts of the state. Today we tend to think that all granite comes from Barre, all marble from Proctor, and all slate from Poultney. In the early days, before the centralization and consolidation of the extractive industries, small quarries, sheds, and mills were quite common. Initially undertaken by local people and woefully undercapitalized, these enterprises were more expressions of hope and speculation than they were sober businesses. Here and there especially fine stone might attract a well established firm; in time that quarry would be absorbed by the larger company. Today the remnants of abandoned quarries can be found in several dozen Vermont towns.

Small or large, centralized or otherwise, the quarries and sheds provided jobs. While native Vermonters took their share of jobs in the developing industries, Scots, Italian, Spanish, Polish, Welsh, and Scandinavian immigrants brought their special skills to Vermont during the latter two decades of the nineteenth and the first decade of the twentieth century. These artistic skills not only enhanced their professional work in the shops, but also carried over into their private lives. Frequently their homes and grounds were decorated with examples of their work.

4-Pat Butter Mold
c. 1929
John Varnum,
Peacham, Vermont
Wood
4½″ L x 4¾″ W x 1″ D
Loaned by the Peacham
Historical Association

2-Pat Butter Mold
c. 1929
John Varnum,
Peacham, Vermont
Wood
2¼″ L x 1¾″ W x ¾″ D
Loaned by the Peacham
Historical Association

Butter Print Mold
c. 1929
John Varnum,
Peacham, Vermont
Wood
3¾" L x 2½" W x ¾" D
Loaned by the Pecham
Historical Association

Milligan Butter Print
c. 1930
George Milligan,
Barnet, Vermont
Wood
5⅜" L x 2¾" W x 3⅜" D
Private collection
   A good example of the
"Hand Print." Milligan's
"Bundle of Grain" was known
as one of his best.

From Generation to Generation

From the 1880's well into the mid 1950's, the Peacham area has been known for its butter prints. In 1879, James R. Kinerson patented a butter printer and mold with a print block frame into which were screwed individual carved print blocks. The print blocks, four or more, divided the butter into desired weights. Kinerson modified the mold of his original patent into the Kinerson Combination Butter Print and began production of his improved design in the early 1880's.

Kinerson had a major influence in the Peacham area and had a number of people carving for him — among them John Varnum and "The Bickford Girls." Shortly after Kinerson's death in 1902, John Varnum purchased the business and was known by store owners as far away as Pittsford as "the finest butter print carver around." For years his carving, as well as the packing and shipping, was done at home. He not only sold locally, but had requests for original designs from New Jersey and California. One of his most intricate molds was made for a special exhibit of prize-winning butter: a cow in two parts, which stood six inches high. Varnum carved butter molds until 1937.

George Milligan and his son George had a butter trunk and print shop, and when George was twelve one of his jobs was to take the prints up to Willow Brook to get them carved. He went up three Saturdays in a row, watching "The Bickford Girls" carving. After that, he decided it was easier and cheaper to try and carve his own. For the next seventy years, he continued to make butter prints, carving on the end grain of birch or maple which he cut from the tree himself.

Both Varnum and Milligan produced Kinerson Combination Butter Prints and both also manufactured and carved the "Hand Print" which was unique to the area and incorporated some of Kinerson's original design. This was a square plunger with a handle and with the print block divided into four or more individual, carved sections. When Milligan carved his last block in 1954, it was the end of an era for a distinctive local tradition. ●

Gravestone
1778
Zerubbabel Collins,
Shaftsbury, Vermont
Marble
32½" H x 19½" W x 2¼" D
Loaned by the Shaftsbury
Historical Society

Gravestone cutting was not
a highly specialized art
in the late 1700's and many
gravestone cutters were also
cabinet makers, wood carvers,
masons, bricklayers and slaters.
Zerubbabel Collins, the son
of a gravestone cutter, Benjamin
Collins of Connecticut, was
a cabinet maker and a carpenter
as well as a gravestone cutter.
He moved to Shaftsbury,
Vermont to be near the source
of marble. When a better grade
of marble was discovered in
Dorset, he moved his family
there. An ornate carver,
Collins frequently used winged
angel heads symbolizing death
and scroll work indicating
the rewards of heaven.

Gravestone
1801
Samuel Dwight,
Arlington, Vermont
Marble
36" L x 20" W x 2" D
Loaned by the Shaftsbury
Historical Society

Samuel Dwight "absconded
to Vermont in 1786 from
Connecticut, leaving his wife
behind. It was in Vermont
between 1790 and 1813 that
Dwight turned to carving
gravestones (after he had failed
as the director of the Clio
Hall School), and examples of
his work can be found in
graveyards throughout
Bennington County. His work
is characterized by the use
of hearts, hands, vines, and
flowers.

Marble Checkerboard
1980
Bernard Nelson,
Proctor, Vermont
Marble
20″ x 20″
Loaned by Bernard Nelson
    Bernie Nelson's parents
came over from Sweden to
work at the Proctor Marble
Company. He was born in
West Rutland and has worked
as a marble setter most of
his life. In his spare time he
builds miniature houses and
log cabins out of marble chips.
He also makes checkerboards.
This particular one he
considers significant because
in making it he used marble
from France, Italy, Tennessee,
Alaska and Vermont.

My Happy Raimbilli Cousins
Gayleen Aiken, Barre, Vermont
Oil
14″ H x 17″ L
Loaned by Don Sunseri
    Gayleen Aiken grew up in
Barre, where she developed
a lifelong interest in the
granite industry. Most of her
youth was spent in and around
the granite sheds, and as
her paintings recollect her
earlier days, it is no surprise
that the granite sheds are a
favorite subject.

My RAIMBILLI HILL COUSINS AND place.

Beyond these specialized artisans and craftsmen with clearly defined skills and fairly
circumscribed work limitations, there was yet
another breed of man, the Yankee tinkerer. Ask
him what he did for a living, and deeply embarrassed, he might mumble some nearly incoherent
response or simply shrug his shoulders. Yet he
was the jack-of-all-trades who did not farm, but
without whom the rural way of life would have
been even more difficult.

This Yankee tinkerer was the man who could
lay up a dry stone wall, build a load of hay, sharpen
saws, jack up the house and put in a new sill,
carve a paddle to replace the broken one in the
churn, dig and stone up a well after dowsing
its proper location, put new handles into old tools,
help out with chores if the farmer was ailing, or
give an extra hand during butchering, corn cutting,
or fence mending time. He also seemed to have
a special knack for fashioning tools or mechan-
isms to do what needed doing, and these were
frequently gems of folk art that today's rural
auctioneers call "primitives" and sell at prices
that would have astounded their makers.

He was not, however, the "hired man," tied to
the daily round of farm chores. His was more likely
a free and independent spirit. Though it was
an economically precarious existence, it enabled
him to "help out" when he was needed, yet it
left him time to locate the best trout pools, tramp
the woods in search of game or herbs, or visit
relatives and friends in the next town or county
should the spirit move.

Slate

Most of the workers who came to the slate quarries of Poultney and Fair Haven were Welshmen from the Penrhyn slate quarries of Caernarvon in northern Wales. They brought with them their skills and artistry. Some proved to be master carvers and practiced their art after a long day in the quarry.

Slate was used first for roofing and then for billiard table tops, mantels, blackboards, tiles, flagging, clock cases, doorsteps and sidewalk squares. After 1850 the "marblizing" of slate began. This process, which caused the finished products to resemble marble, was used chiefly on fancy mantel pieces, fireplaces, flower stands, and clock cases, and was popular through the Victorian period. ●

John Benjamin Evans
(1872-1920)

John Benjamin Evans was born in Cesarea, Wales in 1872 and came to a waiting job in the slate quarries of Poultney in 1906. He brought his wife and small daughter, Maggie, with him, telling his daughter about the big oranges growing in America. As they came by train to their new home he pointed to the pumpkins in the fields, teasing Maggie, "Didn't I tell you they had great big oranges all over America!"

Evans was already an accomplished slate carver and every night after supper he would go out to his shop and by kerosene lantern work until midnight or one o'clock in the morning. Often his daughter would accompany him. "He'd see something that he liked, 'Now, I'd like to make that in stone,' he'd say and he wouldn't have a pattern. He'd just start carving." He used only hand tools: a saw, file or drill for his creations which included such diverse things as the fan (known locally as a "Welsh fan"), a Welsh Bible, a memorial for his parents, a doorstop, a table top, an ink stand and a locket ● for his daughter.

Watercooler
1850-1859
J. and E. Norton,
Bennington, Vermont
Stoneware, cobalt blue
33½" H
Loaned by the
Bennington Museum
   This watercooler was
made for the Hotel Putnam.
The landscape is typical of
the period and is supposed to
be a view of Bennington.

Jug
1850-1859
J. and E. Norton,
Bennington, Vermont
Stoneware, cobalt blue
15" H x 10" Diam.
Loaned by
Mrs. Charlotte T. Blodgett

Butter Crock
1856-59
Nichols and Boynton,
Burlington, Vermont
Stoneware, cobalt blue
7" H x 9" Diam.
Loaned by Lawrence and
Martha Scanlon
   A floral motif is one of the
most common found on
stoneware.

Crock
c. 1827
Monroe MacKenzie,
South Woodstock, Vermont
Stoneware, cobalt blue
10¼" H x 8" D
Courtesy of Hillary Underwood
   South Woodstock pottery was
a short-lived, one-man operation.

Jonathan Fenton was making jugs in Boston in the 1790's and arrived in Dorset, Vermont by 1801. He did not always decorate his jugs but when he did they are usually incised with a fish or an eagle filled in with cobalt blue. It has been suggested that the fish decoration may have been inspired by the good trout fishing in the Mettowee River near Fenton's pottery.

Stoneware

Stoneware came into general usage about 1800 for storage and general household use. Although J. and E. Norton of Bennington was the most famous in Vermont, there were a number of other potteries around the state, those of Fairfax, Burlington, South Woodstock and Dorset being represented in this exhibition.

In terms of folk art it is the cobalt blue decorations on the stoneware that is of most interest. Usually the decoration is simple as in the Burlington and South Woodstock crocks; however, there is one particularly creative artist whose work is characterized by the same sort of dappled or spotted animals, the same fences, and similar trees. His work has been found on Bennington pieces but also on those from West Troy and Fort Edward, New York. Barbara Chiolino suggests that this artist may have been William Leake who left Bennington in 1859 when the Norton potteries were temporarily closed down and, with some other skilled workers from there, went over to West Troy and later to Fort Edward. The watercooler, the spotted lion and the drinking scenes are all examples of this same artist's work.

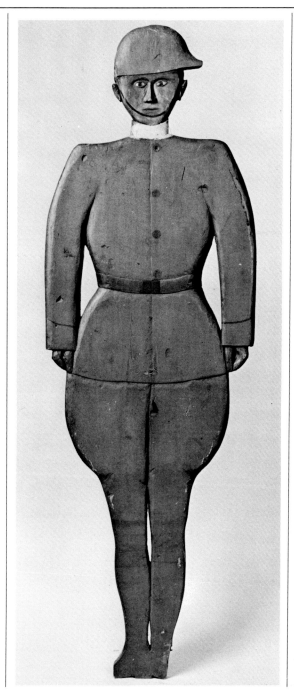

As the decades rolled on and farming gradually declined, occupational opportunities off the farm expanded for both men and women. The urbanization process accelerated; villages became cities and cities became bigger cities even though some retained their organization and status as "towns." Cottage industries either expanded into small manufactories or their proprietors closed them down and went off to work elsewhere. No longer were enlarged villages merely trade centers for the surrounding rural areas; their offices, manufacturing plants, and civic activities generated additional jobs.

Yet even today some strains of Vermont ruralness remain in her people. There is a residue of rural "know how," whether it be love of gardening, the skills of winter driving, or the facile use of the hands in creating useful and artistic objects. There is an appreciation of the natural world and an understanding of the vagaries of the weather. There is still a deep respect for hard work and attendance to duty which makes the characterization "He's a hard worker" about the highest possible accolade.

While many of the non-farm occupations of the nineteenth and early twentieth centuries have become obsolete, it is heartening to recognize that some are being revived in this period of reawakened interest in all things historical, in the values of simple living, and in the appropriate technology.

Weston A. Cate, Jr.
Director,
Vermont Historical Society

Doughboy
c. 1914
Artist unknown,
northern Vermont
Wood, painted
72″ H x 24″ W x 1⅜″ D
Loaned by
Mrs. Hillary Underwood
  This doughboy, locally made in northern Vermont, was used as a recruiting sign outside a church during World War I.

Inn Sign
c. 1780-90
Artist unknown,
Vergennes, Vermont
Wood, painted
49½" H x 31" L
Loaned by Bill Benton
   This was a trade sign for
the Phineas Brown Inn.

Folk Art:
Another Look

Another Look

Within the economies of folk societies of the pre-industrial kind, units of production are self-contained. The units either are single individuals and families producing goods for the family and local neighborhood, or consist of loosely organized groups making products for the village or local district. In other words, home manufacture supplemented with goods made in simple mills and shops supply the needs of folk groups.

Determining which of the artifacts of folk societies are folk art, and which are not, is difficult. There does not seem to be a model by which folk art can be defined other than randomly through personal inclination and intuitions.

The more two-dimensional the folk artifact, seemingly the easier it is for it to achieve recognition as an art form. Paintings and stencilling, quilts and coverlets and weathervanes, for example, all qualify. It would seem that flat objects incorporating familiar visual representations or series of abstract patterns fit rather easily into the definition of folk art.

Moving towards more explicitly three-dimensional artifacts which enfold volume, e.g., baskets, decorated and glazed pots, and painted chests, we find that these also are commonly held to be folk art. The subsistence functions of these objects are more obvious than in the group just mentioned, although the aesthetic qualities are still apparent. With three-dimensional objects, however, the craft required in their making is a consideration which must be dealt with. Craft, in creating the form and function of the folk art object, is inseparable from it. To the extent that it is impossible to divorce folk aesthetic values from craft, it is equally impossible to draw hard and fast distinctions defining folk art separately from folk craft.

Two questions are often raised regarding folk art. One is: by what criterion does a folk artifact not qualify as folk art? The second: under what circumstances does a traditional folk art object cease to be so defined? These are very broad questions for which, I believe, we have no satisfactory answers yet. Answers, when they do come, are apt to bring surprises, partly in the discovery of a new range of artifacts accepted as folk art.

I would like to cite two examples which serve to illustrate how very complex the above two questions are. Both examples have to do with an extended range of folk art, a phenomenon which, for lack of a better term, I have called fugitive folk art.

The first example deals with the nature of the folk aesthetic as this is found in the subsistence hand tools upon which everyday life depends in folk societies. Flails, wooden rakes, the miller's wooden shovel, axe handles, snowshoes, canoe paddles, the bent wood device which holds open a sack for filling, butter paddles, wooden carpenter tools such as planes, bit stocks, spokeshaves: there is an endless host of such things.

Fish Scraper
c. 1866
Frank Allen Josselyn,
Plymouth Vermont
Wood
9" L x 2¼" H x ½" D
Loaned by
Mrs. Barbara Chiolino
    After the Civil War, Mr. Frank Josselyn went off to sea "to regain his health." It was during this time that he carved this tool for scaling fish.

Painted Chest
c. 1810
Artist unknown,
Brownington, Vermont
Pine, painted
39" L x 22¾" H x 16¾" D
Private collection
    This is an early and unusual painted decorated chest found on a farm in Brownington that has been in the hands of the same family since the early 1800's. The chest is thought to have been made by a family member. The country Hepplewhite-type scroll foot would probably date the chest after 1800 in northern Vermont. The decoration is unusual although the ornamental border is not unlike some stencilled interiors — note its similarity to the border decoration on the fireboard of the Strong Mansion.

Chair
19th century
Artist unknown, Vermont
Wood and rush
34″ top to floor – seat 12½″
x 20″ – 17″ seat to floor
Loaned by the Vermont
Historical Society

This chair is significant
because it illustrates a folk
artist's interpretation of a
federal style chair.

Blanket Chest

c. 1824
Attributed to Thomas Matteson,
South Shaftsbury, Vermont
Painted pine and/or maple
40″ H x 40″ W x 20″ D
Loaned by Mr. and
Mrs. Henry Reed

This blanket chest has been
attributed to Thomas Matteson
of South Shaftsbury because
it shows many characteristics
of two chests that are signed
by Matteson and three others
that are attributed to him.
Striking similarities are the
stringing and cross-banding,
quarter rounds and dots and
the painted inlaid appearance
of the oval panel on the
apron of the chest. In shape
and size it is all but identical to
the other Matteson four-drawer
chests.

There is a question as to
whether Thomas Matteson
was the maker or the owner
of the signed chests. Because
there were six Thomas
Mattesons sharing the same
name, it makes it impossible
to determine whether one or
two Thomas Mattesons made or
owned the two signed chests.
Local records do not reveal
anyone making furniture for
sale in South Shaftsbury at that
time. Whoever made the
chests was probably a general
woodworker, building houses
and doing ornamental painting
on floors, walls and furniture.
In rural areas of Vermont,
woodworking was not as
highly specialized as in centers
farther south and often styles,
like chests with false drawers,
were made long after they
were no longer in vogue
elsewhere.

Crazy Quilt
Late 19th century
Artist unknown, Vermont
Silk and velvet
68" x 58"
Loaned by Mrs. Philip Johnson

Crazy quilts were popular in Vermont around the turn of the century. They were a means by which a woman could show off her embroidery skills and also use extra scraps of precious silks and velvets which often had a great deal of sentimental value. These quilts were generally made for show and often for special occasions like an engagement or a wedding.

Checkerboard
? late 19th century
Artist unknown,
Cambridge, Vermont
Wood, painted
19¼" H x 16¼" W x 1" D
Loaned by Louie and Rita Masso

This checkerboard is a good example of one that might have been found in the local general store in the late 1880's in Vermont. Game boards were popular home-made items and are well represented not only by checkerboards but by cribbage and crokinole boards and even handmade dominoes.

The structure of these kinds of tools is different from that of objects commonly given the status of folk art. Essentially they are highly specialized devices for the application of human energy in the accomplishment of work. The shapes of tools become so commonplace and taken for granted within their working context that we seldom think to view them outside that context and to ask whether they may have beauty or other qualities than those having to do strictly with their function. In the folk tradition of the handmaking of subsistence tools and implements the elements of beauty, balance and design are not always consciously sought. They are brought to the object through countless generations of craftsmen and women, and they are inherent in the object. In the process, non-essential or dysfunctional physical features are eliminated so that the tool may come to have the best possible fit with its intended use. There is a concentrated background of care and pains taken in the making of the tool which reflects the collective folk aesthetic of many skilled people, each adding his bit to the development of form and material and proper function over the ages.

There is in such tools a stark beauty in the elimination of the non-essential. Looked at as sculpture they are beautiful; the tools are imbued with beauty in the technique of their making and in their finished form even though the elements of the folk artist may be fugitive.

The second case concerns the immemorially old handcraft technology which began to draw to its close between 1750 and 1850. During this period the factory system evolved and slowly replaced handwork. Until the Industrial Revolution got its legs under it there was a critical period in which the new technology was dependent upon the old to get it going. The "Mother Machines" (engine lathe, milling machine, shaper, drill press, boring mill, etc.) had to be invented, perfected and built within the framework and reference points of hand technology.

In working under the older handcrafts system men and women had long been accustomed to adding decorative touches to their work. The structural parts of wagons, threshers, household goods and farm tools were treated to fancy chamfers and bevels, jogs and jowls, painted stripes and floral design. Since the society was folk cultural, these decorations had folk cultured origins. Therefore, as the small manufactories grew during this period, a mixture of the older handwork and new machine work was carried on side by side. Inevitably, the handsome touches and configurations which were the hallmark of handwork were designed and cut into all sorts of goods now beginning to be produced in the emergent factory system.

BICYCLE·LIVERY
REPAIRS DONE
CAREFULLY AND PROMPTLY
CARRIAGE
AND
PAINT SHOP
A.T. THIBAULT

AMERICAN SEAL
HOUSE PAINTS

M. Anne   Grand-père   Employé   Agnès   Papa
           Nolin   Thibault

Lieu de naissance des Soeurs Th[...]

29 rue Catherine St

1902

Bicycle Sign
1895
Amideé T. Thibault,
St. Albans, Vermont
Wood and highwheeled
Columbia bicycle
84" H x 66" W
Loaned by David L. Davies
  Both a wheelwright and a
talented carver, Amideé
Thibault made this trade sign
for his "Bicycle, Livery and
Carriage Shop and Paint
Shop."

Parade Wagon
1902
Amideé T. Thibault,
St. Albans, Vermont
Wood, paint
Courtesy of Agnes Thibault

Amideé Thibault
1865-1961

Amideé Thibault was born in North Stanbridge, Quebec in 1865 and had little schooling because his father needed him to work his brickyard. In his early years the family moved from Quebec to Manchester, New Hampshire where there was another brickyard, and then back to Quebec. By the age of seventeen, he was helping his uncle make crosses for the Temperance Society of the Parish of Notre Dame de Stanbridge and also helping him do the carving on the pews of the church. Shortly after this, he ran away to Montreal where he learned to do iron work. But money was short and he apparently returned to the brickyard for a brief stint. It was during this time that he began making frequent trips to Vermont. By the age of twenty-five he was married and decided to settle in St. Albans, opening a bicycle carriage repair shop. It was for this that he carved his famous bicycle sign. The sign was placed high on the roof and held in place by iron struts. For a time, sign painting was his first work. He did decorative work on carriages — one of his best remembered was a cow on a dairy carriage and the parade wagon shown here. When automobiles came in, Thibault continued to paint them as he had done with carriages and his designs were known for their originality.

Besides his painting, he did a great deal of repair work, both in iron and wood. But he never seemed to lose his creative urge. He carved toys for his seven daughters, animals, birds, bird houses, knives, statues, picture frames — and was in particular demand for his weathervanes. One of his daughters tells of his pointing them out to her. Today, with the passage of time, only a few are still attributed to him, among them a rooster and a horse.

When bicycles and carriages declined in popularity, Thibault sold and repaired furniture, did carpentry, watch and jewelry repair. He was truly a jack of all trades, but it is chiefly through his carving that his artistry lives on. ●

Take, for instance, William Samson's threshers made in East Berkshire, Vermont in the 1870's: the colorful red and blue paint, picked out with yellow hand-striping and simple floral decoration, complements the profuse chamfering of the wooden parts. Or consider the graceful cast steel thumb screw ornamented with leaves cast in relief, found on an 1870's jointer in a mill in Barnet, Vermont. Its shape is a reverse image of the handforged thumb screws in use in Colonial times and is very beautiful. The cast iron body of this machine is decorated with colorful and nicely done striping and flowers on a deep green background.

Such objects are unique and represent two diametrically opposed areas of human endeavor which met and merged for a few decades. Objects with this kind of hand painted, chamfered, stencilled, forged and cast decoration will never again, in countries like the United States, be produced as articles of easily obtainable, everyday commerce.

Such artifacts were carry-overs from the time when all objects made by mankind were extensions of the human hand, one step removed from the psyche. It was still possible for artisans to imprint at least a part of the vision in their minds in direct, tangible form upon the surface and structure of the material being worked. As the 1800's wore on, the time came when these remnants of fugitive folk decoration became too expensive to apply to what had become the factory production of goods; time had become money.

A curious reversal now occurred as machine technology burgeoned. From the 1850's on into the teens of this century the technology of the Machine, especially of the Mother Machines, came to acquire a strangely compelling mystique of its own. This evolved from the growing body of empirical knowledge shared among machinist craftsmen before it was systematized into written and tablature form by those who became the engineers and technicians of the new age.

The machine craftsmen's aesthetic increasingly came to be centered in the heavily ornamented, glistening iron and steel and brass of the machines themselves and in the body of esoteric lore which became the common property of those who shared in their making and in their efficient operation. In those days the older handcraftsman, and whatever remained of the diminished stream of his folk art continuum, lived on in the machinist and his apprentice. The earlier craftsman had made things direct from his own mind and hand. The early machinist centered his energies in developing and making a complex of machines, hidden away in factories it is true, but as strikingly decorative in their own way as anything which had gone before.

These men and their apprentices are gone in their turn. Today the infinitely specialized machine is supreme and men are its mere appurtenances. What we can buy today are floods of arithmetically determined goods, as alike as peas in a pod, which bear no traces of the human hand upon their surfaces.

Sandy Ives, folklorist, has said, "Ninety-eight percent of the world's aesthetic theory is based on two percent of human aesthetic experience."[1] I take this to mean that ninety-eight percent of human aesthetic experience springs from the millions of unknown people whose art has been a functioning and inseparable part of their daily lives, and all of whom have lived beneath the notice of recorded history. Here, in this exhibit of Vermont folk art, one can sense the underlying structure and balance of forces which for a long time prevailed in the lives of a people who lived at the edge of the machine age, whose lives both shaped their sense of beauty and were in turn shaped by it.

Scott E. Hastings, Jr.
Director,
Billings Farm Museum

---

[1]Edward D. Ives,
in a personal communication to the author.

"Green Mountain Boy" Traverse Sled
1905
Clarence J. Poore,
Rutland, Vermont
Painted wood, iron
10'8" L x 12" W x 13" H
Loaned by the
Shelburne Museum

Clarence Poore was a fine woodworker who started when he was about sixteen in the building trade. When he built this sled for his son, he was working in the Rutland Railroad car shop and had access to equipment and material to build the sled. Clarence's father-in-law John L. Edwards, was a sign writer by profession and he painted free-hand the design that is still visible on the sled along with the name of the sled and its owner, his grandson, John E. Poore. The "Green Mountain Boy" saw a lot of use, was known as "one of the best on the hill," and wore out at least one pair of shoes.

139.

Lenders

Robert Bearor
Jane Beck
Bennington Museum
William Benton
Mrs. James Beyor
Billings Farm Museum
Claire Blanchard
Gregg Blasdel
Charlotte T. Blodgett
Mr. and Mrs. William V. N. Carroll
Castleton Historical Society
Charlotte Memorial Museum
Barbara Chiolino
Jane H. Choate
David L. Davies
Joe Duggan
Fairbanks Museum and Planetarium
Mrs. Howard J. Farmer
The Farrar-Mansur House Museum
Suzanne and Howard Feldman
Arlyn W. Foote
Franklin County Museum
Frederick and Mary Fried
Mrs. Raymond Gerow, Sr.
Pruella Gibson
Forrest A. Gray
Rayna Green
Green Mountain Antiques
Thomas E. Hannan
Bessie F. Harlow
Marjorie B. Herrick
Historical Society of Windham County
Hood Museum of Art, Dartmouth College
Lee Hull
Flossie Humphrey
Mrs. Philip Johnson
Edith Temple Jones
Theodore and Rose Lambert
Frederick Lapham III
John Lawyer
Imelda Lepine
Manchester Historical Society
Marlboro Historical Society

Louie and Rita Masso
Florence Mead
Philip B. Meigs
Edmond Menard
Kendra and David Merrill
Duane E. Merrill
Museum of Man, National Museums of Canada
Bernard Nelson
Michael Nemkovich
The Old Stone House Museum
Frank Patoine
Rosa Patoine
Peacham Historical Association
Clare Phillips
Myrtle S. Ray
Mr. and Mrs. Henry Reed
Annette Richards
Seth Rosenbaum
Laurence and Martha Scanlon
Cleland E. Selby
Shaftsbury Historical Society
Shelburne Museum
Sheldon Museum
Tim Stevenson
Louise H. Stiles
John Strong Mansion, D.A.R., Inc.
Don Sunseri
Winston and Isabelle Swain
Sybil Sweet
Perley D. Sweetser
Town of Greensboro
Hillary Underwood
Vermont Historical Society
Marjorie M. Warden
Marilyn Ware
Newton Washburn
Pauline Welch
Elizabeth S. White
Edward S. Whitney
Margaret and Alan Wilcox

Project Staff:

Catalog Designer: Mason Singer, Laughing Bear Associates
Catalog Photographer: Erik Borg
   Assistant Photographer: Katherine Kennedy
Consultants: Kristina Bielenberg
           Gordon Day
           Rayna Green
           Frederick Fried
           Duane Merrill
           Barbara S. Van Vuren
Coordinator of Interpretation: Meg Ostrum
Coordinator of Publicity: Linda Prescott
Curatorial Consultant: Elaine Eff
Exhibit Designer: Daniel Mayer
Fieldworkers: Jane Beck
           Nora Groce
           Kim Guay
           Karen Lane
           John Moody
Project Administrator: Nike Speltz
Project Director: Jane Beck
Typist: Lucille Collins

Selection Committee:

Jane Beck, Vermont Folklorist
David Dangremond, Director, Bennington Museum
Elaine Eff, Curatorial Consultant
Scott Hastings, Director, Billings Farm Museum
William Lipke, Professor of Art History,
   University of Vermont

A Selected Bibliography

Ames, Kenneth L. **Beyond Necessity: Art in the Folk Tradition.** Winterthur, Delaware: Henry Francis du Pont Winterthur Museum, 1977.

Banks, William Nathaniel. "History in Towns: Castleton, Vermont." **Antiques,** January 1978, pp. 158-177.

Bettenhausen, Marge. "Danville Whittler Sends 'Birds' to Astronauts." **Caledonian Record,** St. Johnsbury, Vermont April 9, 1969.

Bielenberg, Kristina L. **The Sweetser Family Basketmakers.** Thesis for Goddard College, 1974.

Black, Patti Carr (Editor). **Made by Hand: Mississippi Folk Art.** Jackson, Mississippi: Department of Archives and History, 1980.

Brasser, Ted J. **A Basketful of Indian Culture Change.** National Museum of Man, Mercury Series, Ottawa, 1975.

Briggs, Mildred. "Historic Wooden Cyclist Might Return." **St. Albans Messenger,** Friday, December 12, 1969.

Buckeye, Nancy. "Samuel Dwight: Stone Carver of Bennington County, Vermont." **Vermont History,** Vol. 43, No. 3, 1975, pp. 208-216.

Cahill, Holger (Editor). **American Folk Art: The Art of the Common Man in America 1750-1900.** New York: Museum of Modern Art, 1932.

Cannon, Hal (Editor). **Utah Folk Art.** Provo, Utah: Brigham Young University Press, 1980.

Chiolino, Barbara. "Early Vermont Stoneware in Vogue." **Sunday Rutland Herald and the Sunday Times Argus, March 26, 1978, Page 5, Sec. 3.**
March 26, 1978, Page 5, Sec. 3.

Chiolino, Barbara. "Folk Art on Utilitarian Stoneware." **Spinning Wheel,** April 1968, pp. 16-18.

Christensen, Erwin D., **Early American Wood Carving.** New York: Dover Publications, Inc., 1972.

Day, Gordon. "Western Abenaki." **Handbook of North American Indians: Northeast** Vol. 15, Washington, D.C. Smithsonian Institution, 1978. pp. 148-159.

Delph, Shirley and John. **New England Decoys.** Exton, Pennsylvania: Schiffer Publishing Ltd., n.d.

Dennis, Lee. "Spruce Gum Boxes: Logging Camp Folk Art." **Spinning Wheel,** May 1975, pp. 20-21.

Earney, Filmore C. "The Slate Industry of Western Vermont." **The Journal of Geography.** Vol. 62, No. 7, October, 1963, pp. 300-310.

Eaton, Allen H. **Handicrafts of New England.** New York: Harper and Bros. Publishers, 1949.

Ericson, Jack T. **Folk Art in America.** Antiques Magazine Library, New York: Mayflower Books, Inc., 1979.

Fales, Jr. Dean A. and Robert Bishop (Editors). **American Painted Furniture 1660-1880.** New York: E. P. Dutton, 1979.

Fendelman, Helaine. **Tramp Art: An Itinerant's Folk Art.** New York: E. P. Dutton & Co. Inc., 1975.

Finn, Maurice L. "His Hobby is Woodcarving." **Vermont Life,** Winter, 1950 pp. 42-43.

Fried, Fred and Mary. **America's Forgotten Folk Arts.** New York: Pantheon Books, 1978.

Grancsay, Stephen V. **The Metropolitan Museum of Art: American Engraved Powder Horns: A Study Based on J. H. Grenville Gilbert Collection.** New York, 1945.

Harding, William. "The Graveyard at Old Benndington, Vermont and the Gravestones." Unpublished MS, February, 1973.

Hebb, Caroline. "A Distinctive Group of Early Vermont Painted Furniture." **Antiques,** September 1973, pp. 458-461.

Hemphill, Jr., Herbert W. **Folk Sculpture U.S.A.** Brooklyn, New York: The Brooklyn Museum, 1976.

Jones, Suzi (Editor). **Webfoots and Bunchgrassers: Folk Art of the Oregon Country.** Salem, Oregon: Oregon Arts Commission, Your Town Press, Inc., 1980.

Levin, Ruth. "The Bennington Museum Says: Daniel Williams Harmon Part I." **Bennington Banner,** Wednesday, September 17, 1980. "Daniel Williams Harmon Part II." **Bennington Banner,** Wednesday, September 24, 1980.

Morrissey, Charles T. **Vermont: A Bicentennial History.** American Association for State and Local History, New York: W. W. Norton, Co., Inc., 1981.

Needham, Walter (told to) Barrows Massey. **A Book of Country Things.** Brattleboro, Vermont: The Stephen Greene Press, 1965.

Newton, Rev. Ephraim H. **The History of Marlborough, Vermont.** Montpelier: Vermont Historical Society, 1930.

Pelletier, Gaby. **Abenaki Basketry.** To be published in the National Museum of Man, Mercury Series, December, 1981.

Cavendish Sampler
1834
Rebekah Saunders,
Cavendish, Vermont
Linen and silk thread
22″ H x 19″ W
Loaned by Suzanne and
Howard Feldman

The alphabet and numerals are typical of samplers, as are such stylized designs as a fruit bowl with two weeping willows on either side. What is interesting about this sampler is that it is done in the form of a family register and covers a span of almost fifty years.

Quimby, Ian M. G. and Scott T. Swank (Editors). **Perspective on American Folk Art**. The Henry Francis du Pont Winterthur Museum. Winterthur, Delaware, New York: W. W. Norton & Co., 1980.

"Records of Passage. Northern New England Illuminated Manuscripts." **Colonial Homes**, May-June, 1981, pp. 74-75.

Reese, Rosemary Sullivan. **Frank Moran: Woodcarver**. MA Thesis Cooperstown Graduate Program, 1975.

Rhodes, Lynette I. **American Folk Art: From the Traditional to the Naive**. Cleveland: The Cleveland Museum of Art, 1978.

Russell, Howard S. **A Long, Deep Furrow**. Hanover, New Hampshire: University Press of New England, 1976.

Safford, Carleton L. and Robert Bishop. **America's Quilts and Coverlets**. New York: E. P. Dutton & Co., Inc., 1980.

Speck, Frank G. **Penobscot Man**. Philadelphia: University of Pennsylvania Press, 1940.

Thompson, Zadock. **History of Vermont: Natural, Civil and Statistical**. Burlington: Chauncey Goodrich, 1842.

Toussaint, Tennie G. "Russell Risley: Faces on a Vermont Barn." **Mad and Magnificent Yankees**, ed. Clarissa Silitch. Dublin, N.H.: Yankee Magazine, 1973.

Watkins, Lura Woodside. **Early New England Potters and Their Wares**. Cambridge: Harvard University, 1950.

Webster, David and William Kehoe. **Decoys at Shelburne Museum**. Shelburne: Published by Shelburne Museum, 1961.

Willard, Larry. "Hermit Woodcarver." **Yankee Magazine**, April 1950, pp. 34-35.

Wilson, Harold Fisher. **The Hill Country of Northern New England**. New York: AMS Press, Inc., 1967.

Always in Season:
Folk Art and Traditional Culture in Vermont

Catalog Design: **The Laughing Bear Associates**
Principal Catalog Photography: **Erik Borg**
Typesetting: **RW Roulston**
Printing and Binding: **Northlight Studio Press**

Vermont Council on the Arts, Inc.
136 State Street
Montpelier, Vermont 05602